WISDOM
FROM THE
OVAL OFFICE

WISDOM FROM THE OVAL OFFICE

WORDS FROM GEORGE WASHINGTON TO THE PRESENT

BY PIERCE WORD

History Publishing Company
Palisades, New York

Copyright©2013 by Pierce Word
Word, Pierce

LCCN: 2013931912
ISBN: 9781933909448 (HC)
   1933909447
ISBN: 9781933909493 (Paper)
   1933909498
ISBN: 9781933909936 (eBook)
   1933909935
SAN: 850-5942

Word, Pierce.

   Wisdom from the Oval Office : Words from
George Washington to the Present / by Pierce Word. --
1st ed. -- Palisades, NY
: History Pub. Co., c2013.

      p. ; cm.

      ISBN: 978-1-933909-44-8 (HC) ; 978-1-933909-93-6
(eBook)
      Includes bibliographical references and index.
      Summary: The largest collection of presidential
quotations ever assembled: 40 chapters, each dealing
with one of the major themes of life. It comprises
a broad range of political perspective, covering
universal truth, human behavior, and even
love.--Publisher.

      1. Presidents--United States--Quotations.
   2. United States--Politics and
government--Quotations, maxims, etc.
   3. Leadership--Quotations, maxims, etc. I. Title.

E176.1 .W67 2013   2013931912
352.23/80973--dc23   1305

Published in the United States of America by
History Publishing Company, LLC
Palisades, New York
Printed in the United States on acid-free paper
First Edition

A WORD TO THE READER

"Knowledge comes, but wisdom lingers."
—Calvin Coolidge

Wisdom from the Oval Office introduces readers to a wide collection of quotes from all forty-three U.S. presidents (forty-four, if Grover Cleveland's two separate presidencies are included), all organized by life's major themes, such as Love, Politics, Success, Time, and Wisdom. While one target market is the student, who will find this book a handy, easily accessible reference, this book is also perfect for readers interested in learning more about our presidents' perspectives on life, as revealed in their quotations.

Unlike other quotation books, which can be somewhat dry, *Wisdom from the Oval Office* offers a vibrant collection that will amuse, inspire, and enlighten. It is arranged for quick access, with quotations located under alphabetically organized topics, with a comprehensive index for speedy access.

Wisdom from the Oval Office consists of forty chapters, each dealing with one of life's major themes. These categories were chosen from a wide range of possible topics, and were gathered from search engines, forums, and library catalogs. The next step was to see how many presidents had actually quoted within these categories. The final result—a compilation of the largest collection of presidential quotations to date!

I sincerely hope the reader will have as much pleasure reading this book as I had in compiling this work of honor.

Pierce Word
September 1, 2012
Chicago, Illinois

TABLE OF CONTENTS

Chapter One	**America**	1
Chapter Two	**Belief**	20
Chapter Three	**Business**	24
Chapter Four	**Change**	28
Chapter Five	**Constitution**	32
Chapter Six	**Country**	41
Chapter Seven	**Democracy**	50
Chapter Eight	**Economy**	58
Chapter Nine	**Education**	63
Chapter Ten	**Error**	69
Chapter Eleven	**Freedom**	72
Chapter Twelve	**Friendship**	84
Chapter Thirteen	**God**	95
Chapter Fourteen	**Government**	101
Chapter Fifteen	**Happiness**	122
Chapter Sixteen	**History**	127
Chapter Seventeen	**Honor**	134
Chapter Eighteen	**Hope**	137
Chapter Nineteen	**Law**	142
Chapter Twenty	**Leadership**	148

Chapter Twenty-One **Liberty** 153

Chapter Twenty-Two **Life** 161

Chapter Twenty-Three **Love** 171

Chapter Twenty-Four **Mind** 174

Chapter Twenty-Five **Money** 180

Chapter Twenty-Six **Office** 185

Chapter Twenty-Seven **Peace** 191

Chapter Twenty-Eight **Politics** 199

Chapter Twenty-Nine **Power** 208

Chapter Thirty **Presidency** 216

Chapter Thirty-One **Religion** 229

Chapter Thirty-Two **Rights** 234

Chapter Thirty-Three **Success** 240

Chapter Thirty-Four **Time** 244

Chapter Thirty-Five **Trust** 248

Chapter Thirty-Six **Truth** 252

Chapter Thirty-Seven **War** 259

Chapter Thirty-Eight **Wisdom** 269

Chapter Thirty-Nine **Wish** 274

Chapter Forty **World** 279

Index 293

CHAPTER ONE

America

George Washington

"The time is near at hand which must determine whether Americans are to be free men or slaves."
   —Address to Continental Army before Battle of Long Island. August 27, 1776.

"Someday, following the example of the United States of America, there will be a United States of Europe."
   —Collection of Letters to Marquis Lafayette. 1777-1799.

"The name 'American' must always exalt the just pride of patriotism."
   —Farewell Address. September 19, 1796.

"The preservation of the sacred fire of liberty and the destiny of the republican model of government are entrusted to the hands of the American people."
   —Inaugural Address. April 30, 1789.

John Adams

"All the perplexities, confusion and distress in America arise, not from defects in their Constitution or Confederation, not from want of honor or virtue, so much as from the downright ignorance of the nature of coin, credit and circulation."
　　—Letter to Thomas Jefferson. August 23, 1787.

"I always consider the settlement of America with reverence and wonder, as the opening of a grand scene and design in providence, for the illumination of the ignorant and the emancipation of the slavish part of mankind all over the earth."
　　—In His *A Dissertation on the Canon and Feudal Law* (1765).

Thomas Jefferson

"If there is one principle more deeply rooted in the mind of every American, it is that we should have nothing to do with conquest."
　　—Letter to William Short. July 28, 1791.

"Peace and abstinence from European interferences are our objects, and so will continue while the present order of things in America remains uninterrupted."
　　—Letter to DuPont De Nemours. April 1802.

"I predict future happiness for Americans if they can prevent the government from wasting the labors of the people under the pretense of taking care of them."
　　—Reported by Stephen D. Hanson in
　　　Transcending Time with Thomas Jefferson (2010).[1]

"I am mortified to be told that, in the United States of America, the sale of a book can become a subject of inquiry and of criminal inquiry too."
　　—Letter to Nicolas Gouin Dufief. April 19, 1814.

James Madison

"The Constitution preserves the advantage of being armed which Americans possess over the people of almost every other nation where the governments are afraid to trust the people with arms."
—*The Federalist*. January 29, 1788.[2]

"America was indebted to immigration for her settlement and prosperity. That part of America which had encouraged them most had advanced most rapidly in population, agriculture and the arts."
—Motion to the House of Representatives, as reported by John Sanderson in *Views and Opinions of American Statesmen* (1856).

John Q. Adams

"America does not go abroad in search of monsters to destroy."
—Independence Day Address. July 4, 1821.

"The highest glory of the American Revolution was this: it connected in one indissoluble bond the principles of civil government with the principles of Christianity."
—Independence Day Address. July 4, 1821.

Andrew Jackson

"Americans are not a perfect people, but we are called to a perfect mission."
—Remark on His Assassination Attempt. January 30, 1835.[3]

James Buchanan

"Prevent the American people from crossing the Rocky Mountains? You might as well command Niagara not to flow. We must fulfill our destiny."
—Speech to Congress. December 4th, 1843.

Abraham Lincoln

"My dream is of a place and a time where America will once again be seen as the last best hope of earth."
   —Second Annual Message. December 1, 1862.[4]

"America will never be destroyed from the outside. If we falter and lose our freedoms, it will be because we destroyed ourselves."
   —Address before the Young Men's Lyceum of Springfield, Illinois. January 27, 1838.[5]

Grover Cleveland

"I know there is a Supreme Being who rules the affairs of men and whose goodness and mercy have always followed the American people, and I know He will not turn from us now if we humbly and reverently seek His powerful aid."
   —Inaugural Address. March 4, 1893.

"A truly American sentiment recognizes the dignity of labor and the fact that honor lies in honest toil."
   —Letter Accepting Nomination of the U.S. Presidency. August, 18, 1884.

Benjamin Harrison

"We Americans have no commission from God to police the world."
   —Statement to Congress in 1888.[6]

Theodore Roosevelt

"The things that will destroy America are prosperity-at-any-price, peace-at-any-price, safety-first instead of duty-first, the love of soft living, and the get-rich-quick theory of life."
   —Letter to S. Stanwood Menken. January 10, 1917.

"A typical vice of American politics is the avoidance of saying anything real on real issues."
—*The Outlook.* July 27, 1912.

"We can have no "50-50" allegiance in this country. Either a man is an American and nothing else, or he is not an American at all."
—Speech in Pittsburg, Pennsylvania. July 27, 1917.

"To announce that there must be no criticism of the president is morally treasonable to the American public."
—*Kansas City Star.* May 7, 1918.

"The American people abhor a vacuum."
—Speech in Cairo, Illinois. October 3, 1907.

William Taft

"If humor be the safety of our race, then it is due largely to the infusion into the American people of the Irish brain."
—Address in Hot Springs, Virginia. August 5, 1908.

"Anti-Semitism is a noxious weed that should be cut out. It has no place in America."
—Address to the Anti-Defamation League in Chicago, Illinois. December, 23, 1920.

Woodrow Wilson

"America is not anything if it consists of each of us. It is something only if it consists of all of us."
—Speech in Pittsburgh, Pennsylvani. January 29, 1916.

"The American Revolution was a beginning, not a consummation."
—Address to The National Society Of The Daughters Of The American Revolution, Washington, D.C. October, 11, 1915.

"America lives in the heart of every man everywhere who wishes to find a region where he will be free to work out his destiny as he chooses."
—Campaign Speech, Chicago, Illinois. April 6, 1912.

"America is the only idealistic nation in the world."
—Address at Sioux Falls. September 8, 1919.

"Property as compared with humanity, as compared with the red blood in the American people, must take second place, not first place."
—"Human Rights" Speech in Parade Grounds, Minneapolis, Minnesota. September 18, 1912.

"Neutrality is a negative word. It does not express what America ought to feel. We are not trying to keep out of trouble; we are trying to preserve the foundations on which peace may be rebuilt."
—Address To The National Society Of The Daughters Of The American Revolution, Washington, D.C. October, 11, 1915.

"America was established not to create wealth but to realize a vision, to realize an ideal—to discover and maintain liberty among men."
—Speech to Chicago Democrat's Iroquois Club. February 12, 1912.

"Sometimes people call me an idealist. Well, that is the way I know I am an American."
—Address at Sioux Falls. September 8, 1919.

Warren Harding

"I don't know much about Americanism, but it's a damn good word with which to carry an election."
—Speech in 1919.[7]

"The success of our popular government rests wholly upon the correct interpretation of the deliberate, intelligent, dependable popular will of America."
—Inaugural Address. March 4, 1921.

"America's present need is not heroics, but healing; not nostrums, but normalcy; not revolution, but restoration; not agitation, but adjustment; not surgery, but serenity; not the dramatic, but the dispassionate; not experiment, but equipoise; not submergence in internationality, but sustainment in triumphant nationality."
—Speech in Boston, Massachusetts. May 24, 1920.

Calvin Coolidge

"After all, the chief business of the American people is business. They are profoundly concerned with producing, buying, selling, investing and prospering in the world."
—Speech to the American Society of Newspaper Editors. January 17, 1925.

"To live under the American Constitution is the greatest political privilege that was ever accorded to the human race."
—Address at the White House. December 12, 1924.

"Patriotism is easy to understand in America. It means looking out for yourself by looking out for your country."
—Memorial Day Speech in Northampton, Massachusetts. May 30, 1923.

Herbert Hoover

"There are only two occasions when Americans respect privacy, especially in Presidents. Those are prayer and fishing."
—*Let's Go Fishin'*. April 22, 1943.

"In America today, we are nearer a final triumph over poverty than in any other land."
    —Address at Madison Square Garden in New York City. October 31, 1932.

"No greater nor more affectionate honor can be conferred on an American than to have a public school named after him."
    —Remarks at Dedication of Herbert Hoover Junior High School, San Francisco, California. June 5, 1956.

"America—a great social and economic experiment, noble in motive and far-reaching in purpose."
    —Republican Nomination Acceptance Speech in Palo Alto, California. August 11, 1928.

Franklin Roosevelt

"The school is the last expenditure upon which America should be willing to economize."
    —Campaign Address at Kansas City, Missouri. October 13, 1936.

"I pledge you, I pledge myself, to a new deal for the American people."
    —Nomination Address. July, 2, 1932.

"There is a mysterious cycle in human events. To some generations much is given. Of other generations much is expected. This generation of Americans has a rendezvous with destiny."
    —Speech to the Democratic National Convention in Philadelphia, Pennsylvania. June 27, 1936.

"If we can boondoggle ourselves out of this depression, that word is going to be enshrined in the hearts of the American people for years to come."
    —Speech to the New Jersey State Emergency Council, Newark. January 18, 1936.

"Nobody will ever deprive the American people of the right to vote except the American people themselves and the only way they could do this is by not voting."
—Radio Address from the White House. October 5, 1944.

"Here is my principle: Taxes shall be levied according to ability to pay. That is the only American principle."
—Address at Worcester, Massachusetts. October 21, 1936.

"The overwhelming majority of Americans are possessed of two great qualities: a sense of humor and a sense of proportion."
—Speech in Savannah. November 18, 1933.

Harry Truman

"When even one American—who has done nothing wrong—is forced by fear to shut his mind and close his mouth—then all Americans are in peril."
—Address at the Dedication of the New Washington Headquarters of the American Legion. August 14, 1951.

"You know that being an American is more than a matter of where your parents came from. It is a belief that all men are created free and equal and that everyone deserves an even break."
—'Rear Platform and Other Informal Remarks' in Indiana and Ohio. October 26, 1948.

"I've said many a time that I think the Un-American Activities Committee in the House of Representatives was the most un-American thing in America!"
—Third Radner Lecture, Columbia University, New York City. April 29, 1959.

"America was not built on fear. America was built on courage, on imagination and an unbeatable determination to do the job at hand."
—Special Message to the Congress: The President's First Economic Report. January 8, 1947.

Dwight Eisenhower

"I can think of nothing more boring for the American people than to have to sit in their living rooms for a whole half hour looking at my face on their television screens."
    —*Esquire* (1983).[8]

"There is nothing wrong with America that faith, love of freedom, intelligence, and energy of her citizens cannot cure."
    —*Life* (1969).[9]

"I deplore the need or the use of troops anywhere to get American citizens to obey the orders of constituted courts."
    —The President's News Conference. May 14, 1958.

"I have found out in later years that we were very poor, but the glory of America is that we didn't know it then."
    —*U.S. News & World Report* (1955).[10]

"I have one yardstick by which I test every major problem—and that yardstick is: Is it good for America?"
    —Radio and Television Address to the American People on the Farm Bill Veto. April 16, 1956.

"Whatever America hopes to bring to pass in the world must first come to pass in the heart of America."
    —Inaugural Address. January 20, 1953.

"Only Americans can hurt America."
    —United States Naval Institute: *Proceedings* (1963).[11]

"Here in America we are descended in blood and in spirit from revolutionists and rebels—men and women who dare to dissent from accepted doctrine. As their heirs, may we never confuse honest dissent with disloyal subversion?"
    —Speech at Columbia University's Bicentennial.
        May 31, 1954.

John Kennedy

"The path we have chosen for the present is full of hazards, as all paths are. The cost of freedom is always high, but Americans have always paid it. And there is one path we shall never choose, and that is the path of surrender."
—Radio and Television Report to the American People on the Soviet Arms Buildup in Cuba. October 22, 1962.

"America has tossed its cap over the wall of space."
—Remarks in San Antonio at the Dedication of the Aerospace Medical Health Center. November 21, 1963.

"And so, my fellow Americans, ask not what your country can do for you; ask what you can do for your country."
—Inaugural Address. January 20, 1961.

"We are not afraid to entrust the American people with unpleasant facts, foreign ideas, alien philosophies, and competitive values. For a nation that is afraid to let its people judge the truth and falsehood in an open market, is a nation that is afraid of its people."
—Remarks on the 20th Anniversary of the Voice of America. February 26, 1962.

"I hope that no American will waste his franchise and throw away his vote by voting either for me or against me solely on account of my religious affiliation. It is not relevant."
—*Time* (1960).[12]

"I look forward to a great future for America—a future in which our country will match its military strength with our moral restraint, its wealth with our wisdom, its power with our purpose."
—Remarks at Amherst College upon Receiving an Honorary Degree. October 26, 1963.

"No one has been barred on account of his race from fighting or dying for America, there are no white or colored signs on the foxholes or graveyards of battle."
—Special Message to the Congress on Civil Rights and Job Opportunities. June 19, 1963.

"Let the word go forth from this time and place, to friend and foe alike, that the torch has been passed to a new generation of Americans."
—Inaugural Address. January 20, 1961.

Lyndon Johnson

"They call upon us to supply American boys to do the job that Asian boys should do."
—Remarks in New York City before the American Bar Association. August 12, 1964

"I am a free man, an American, a United States Senator, and a Democrat, in that order."
—*Democratic Digest* (1960).[13]

"I report to you that our country is challenged at home and abroad: that it is our will that is being tried and not our strength; our sense of purpose and not our ability to achieve a better America."
—State of the Union Address (1968).

"I'm tired. I'm tired of feeling rejected by the American people."
—*Philippines Free Press* (1971).[14]

"If the American people don't love me, their descendants will."
—*Time*. October 14, 1974.

"We are not about to send American boys nine or ten thousand miles away from home to do what Asian boys ought to be doing for themselves."
—Remarks in Memorial Hall, Akron University. October 21, 1964.

"This private unity of public men and their God is an enduring source of reassurance for the people of America."
—*Liberty: A Magazine of Religious Freedom* (1965).[15]

"This is not Johnson's war. This is America's war. If I drop dead tomorrow, this war will still be with you."
—Remark in White House Oval Office. October 13, 1967.

"It is the genius of our Constitution that under its shelter of enduring institutions and rooted principles there is ample room for the rich fertility of American political invention."
—Annual Message to the Congress on the State of the Union. January 12, 1966.

Richard Nixon

"No event in American history is more misunderstood than the Vietnam War. It was misreported then, and it is misremembered now."
—*No More Vietnams* (1985).

"I would like to address a few special words to the American people: Your steadfastness in supporting our insistence on peace with honor has made peace with honor possible."
—Address to the Nation Announcing Conclusion of an Agreement on Ending the War and Restoring Peace in Vietnam. January 23, 1973.

"The American people are entitled to see the president and to hear his views directly, and not to see him only through the press."
—The President's News Conference. December 10, 1970.

"Tonight—to you, the great silent majority of my fellow Americans—I ask for your support."
—Address to the Nation on the War in Vietnam.
November 3, 1969.

Gerald Ford

"My fellow Americans, our long national nightmare is over."
—Remarks on Taking the Oath of Office. August 9, 1974.

"The political lesson of Watergate is this: Never again must America allow an arrogant, elite guard of political adolescents to by-pass the regular party organization and dictate the terms of a national election."
—*National Journal Reports.* Government Research
Corporation (1975).[16]

"The three-martini lunch is the epitome of American efficiency. Where else can you get an earful, a bellyful and a snootful at the same time?"
—Remarks to the National Restaurant Association,
Chicago, Illinois. May 28, 1978.

Jimmy Carter

"America did not invent human rights. In a very real sense human rights invented America."
—Farewell Address to the Nation.
January 14, 1981.

"What has happened at Guantanamo Bay does not represent the will of the American people. I'm embarrassed about it, I think it's wrong. I think it does give terrorists an unwarranted excuse to use the despicable means to hurt innocent people."
—Speech in Birmingham, England. July 30, 2005.

Ronald Reagan

"All great change in America begins at the dinner table."
—Farewell Address to the Nation. January 11, 1989.

"It is time to restore the American precept that each individual is accountable for his actions."
—Republican National Convention Miami, Florida.
July 31, 1968.

"Today we did what we had to do. They counted on America to be passive. They counted wrong."
—Address to the Nation on the United States Air Strike Against Libya. April 14, 1986.

"My fellow Americans, I am pleased to tell you I just signed legislation which outlaws Russia forever. The bombing begins in five minutes."
—Joking during a Microphone Check. August 11, 1984.

"While I take inspiration from the past, like most Americans, I live for the future."
—Address to the Republican National Convention in Houston. August 17, 1992.

"Drug abuse is a repudiation of everything America is."
—Address to the Nation on the Campaign Against Drug Abuse. September 14, 1986.

George H. W. Bush

"We don't want an America that is closed to the world. What we want is a world that is open to America."
   —Remarks at the Swearing-in Ceremony for Carla A. Hills as United States Trade Representative. February 6, 1989.

"America is never wholly herself unless she is engaged in high moral principle. We as a people have such a purpose today. It is to make kinder the face of the nation and gentler the face of the world."
   —Inaugural Address. January 20, 1989.

Bill Clinton

"When we make college more affordable, we make the American dream more achievable."
   —Remarks on Launching the Agenda for Higher Education and Lifetime Learning. January 20, 2000.

"There is nothing wrong with America that cannot be cured with what is right in America."
   —First Inaugural Address, Washington, D.C. January 20, 1993.

"America does not need a religious war. It needs reaffirmation of the values that for most of us are rooted in our religious faith."
   —Remarks at the University of Notre Dame, South Bend, Indiana. September 11, 1992.

George W. Bush

"Hundreds of thousands of American servicemen and women are deployed across the world in the war on terror. By bringing hope to the oppressed, and delivering justice to the violent, they are making America more secure."
   —State of the Union. Address January 20, 2004.

"If America shows weakness and uncertainty, the world will drift toward tragedy. That will not happen on my watch."
—Remarks to the Republican Governors Association. February 23, 2004.

"America will never seek a permission slip to defend the security of our people."
—State of the Union Address. January 20, 2004.

"Terrorist attacks can shake the foundations of our biggest buildings, but they cannot touch the foundation of America. These acts shatter steel, but they cannot dent the steel of American resolve."
—Address to the Nation. September 11, 2001.

"I believe the most solemn duty of the American president is to protect the American people."
—Remarks Accepting the Presidential Nomination at the Republican National Convention in New York City. September 2, 2004.

"I will never relent in defending America—whatever it takes."
—Remarks in Columbus, Ohio. September 1, 2004.

"You work three jobs? Uniquely American, isn't it?"
—Remarks in a Discussion on Strengthening Social Security in Omaha, Nebraska. February 4, 2005.

"America must not ignore the threat gathering against us."
—Address to the Nation on Iraq, Cincinnati, Ohio. October 7, 2002

"America is a Nation with a mission—and that mission comes from our most basic beliefs. We have no desire to dominate, no

ambitions of empire. Our aim is a democratic peace—a peace founded upon the dignity and rights of every man and woman."
—State of the Union Address. January 20, 2004.

"America is the land of the second chance."
—The 2004 State of the Union Address. January 20, 2004.

Barack Obama

"That is the true genius of America, a faith in the simple dreams of its people, the insistence on small miracles. That we can say what we think; write what we think, without hearing a sudden knock on the door. That we can have an idea and start our own business without paying a bribe or hearing a sudden knock on the door. That we can participate in the political process without fear of retribution, and that our votes will be counted-or at least, most of the time."
—Speech at the Democratic National Convention.
July 27, 2004.

"There are patriots who opposed the war in Iraq and there are patriots who supported the war in Iraq. We are one people, all of us pledging allegiance to the stars and stripes, all of us defending the United States of America."
—Speech at the Democratic National Convention.
July 27, 2004.

"They would give me an African name, Barack, or blessed, believing that in a tolerant America your name is no barrier to success."
—Speech at the Democratic National Convention.
July 27, 2004.

"There is not a liberal America and a conservative America—there is the United States of America."

"There is not a Black America and a White America and Latino America and Asian America—there's the United States of America."
 —Speech at the Democratic National Convention.
  July 27, 2004.

"Americans still believe in an America where anything's possible—they just don't think their leaders do."
 —Speech at the "Take Back America" Conference,
  Washington D.C. June 13, 2006.

"The United States has been enriched by Muslim Americans. Many other Americans have Muslims in their families or have lived in a Muslim-majority country—I know, because I am one of them."
 —Remarks to the Grand National Assembly of Turkey in
  Ankara. April 6, 2009.

1 Pg. 125. Stephen D. Hanson, *Transcending Time with Thomas Jefferson* (2010).
2 No. 46.
3 Although the veracity of this quote is attested to by several scholars, contention to its authenticity is still prevalent. January 30, 1835.
4 Paraphrased: V. 153, Pt. 12, June 18, 2007 to June 26, 2007. edited by Congress (U.S.).
5 *Congressional Record*, May 19, 2005. Whether these exact words were uttered in the Lyceum Speech is debatable; however, it does accurately embody the sentiment of the said event.
6 Caroline T. Hamsberger, *Treasury of Presidential Quotations* (1964).
7 It is argued that this was actually an exchange of words between journalist Talcott Williams and Senator Boies Penrose. Speech of 1919.
8 Vol. 100. *Esquire* Magazine (1983).
9 Vol. 66, no. 13. *Life* Magazine (1969).
10 Vol. 39. *U.S. News & World Report* (1955).
11 Vol. 89. *Proceedings* United States Naval Institute (1963).
12 Vol. 76. *Time* (1960).
13 Vol. 7. Democratic National Committee (U.S.). *Democratic Digest*, (1960).
14 Vol. 64. *Philippines Free Press* (1971).
15 Vols. 60-62. Religious Liberty Bureau, Religious Liberty Association (Washington, D.C.). *Liberty: a Magazine of Religious Freedom* (1965).
16 Vol. 7. *National Journal Reports*. Government Research Corporation (1975).

CHAPTER TWO

Belief

Thomas Jefferson

"To compel a man to furnish funds for the propagation of ideas he disbelieves and abhors is sinful and tyrannical."
—*A Bill for Establishing Religious Freedom* (1779).[1]

"An enemy generally says and believes what he wishes."
—Letter to Mr. Dumas. March 29, 1788.

"Ignorance is preferable to error, and he is less remote from the truth who believes nothing than he who believes what is wrong."
—Letter to Mr. Dumas. March 29, 1788.

"It is always better to have no ideas than false ones; to believe nothing, than to believe what is wrong."
—Letter to James Madison. July 19, 1788.

Andrew Jackson

"Any man worth his salt will stick up for what he believes right,

but it takes a slightly better man to acknowledge instantly and without reservation that he is in error."
—Quoted by Randy Okray in *Crew Resource Management for the Fire Service* (2004).[2]

Abraham Lincoln

"I am a firm believer in the people. If given the truth, they can be depended upon to meet any national crisis."
—Speech to House of Representatives. January 12, 1848.[3]

"The probability that we may fail in the struggle ought not to deter us from the support of a cause we believe to be just."
—Speech in the Hall of the House of Representatives, Springfield, Illinois. December 20, 1839.

Theodore Roosevelt

"Believe you can and you're halfway there."
—U.S. Congress, *Congressional Record.* October 9, 2007.[4]

Franklin Roosevelt

"We have always held to the hope, the belief, the conviction that there is a better life, a better world, beyond the horizon."
—Address. Oct. 12, 1940.

Harry Truman

"You know that being an American is more than a matter of where your parents came from. It is a belief that all men are created free and equal and that everyone deserves an even break."
—'Rear Platform and Other Informal Remarks' in Indiana and Ohio. October 26, 1948.

"You can always amend a big plan, but you can never expand a

little one. I don't believe in little plans."
—Remarks to the American Society of Civil Engineers.
November 2, 1949.

Dwight Eisenhower

"I like to believe that people in the long run are going to do more to promote peace than our governments."
—Radio and Television Broadcast with Prime Minister Macmillan in London. August 31, 1959.

Lyndon Johnson

"I believe the destiny of your generation—and your nation—is a rendezvous with excellence."
—Remarks upon presenting the First Presidential Scholars Awards. June 10, 1964.

"What convinces is conviction. Believe in the argument you're advancing. If you don't you're as good as dead."
—Often-Said Remark. *The Years of Lyndon Johnson: Master of the Senate* (2002).

Jimmy Carter

"We become not a melting pot but a beautiful mosaic. Different people, different beliefs, different yearnings, different hopes, different dreams."
—Department of Health, Education, and Welfare Remarks and a Question-and-Answer Session with Department Employees. February 16, 1977.

George W. Bush

"I believe the most solemn duty of the American president is to protect the American people."

—Remarks accepting the Presidential Nomination at the Republican National Convention in New York City. September 2, 2004.

"America is a Nation with a mission—and that mission comes from our most basic beliefs. We have no desire to dominate, no ambitions of empire. Our aim is a democratic peace—a peace founded upon the dignity and rights of every man and woman."
—Address before a Joint Session of the Congress on the State of the Union. January 20, 2004.

Barack Obama

"My parents shared not only an improbable love; they shared an abiding faith in the possibilities of this nation. They would give me an African name, Barack, or blessed, believing that in a tolerant America your name is no barrier to success."
—Speech at the Democratic National Convention July 27, 2004.

"Americans still believe in an America where anything's possible."
—Speech at the 'Take Back America' Conference, Washington D.C. June 13, 2006.

---

1   Ch. 82.
2   Pg. 25. Some scholars argue this quote is actually attributed to General Peyton C. March. *Crew Resource Management for the Fire Service* (2004) by Randy Okray.
3   Although this particular quote is also said to be attributed to Douglas MacArthur, the quote matches the sentiment of Lincoln's speech.
4   Vol. 153, pt. 19. U.S. Congress, *Congressional Record*. October 9, 2007.

CHAPTER THREE

Business

George Washington

"Let your Discourse with Men of Business be short and Comprehensive."
  —Said of Washington by Lyndon Johnson to the Members of the U.S. Chamber of Commerce. April 27, 1964.

Andrew Jackson

"The duty of government is to leave commerce to its own capital and credit as well as all other branches of business, protecting all in their legal pursuits, granting exclusive privileges to none."
  —Letter to William Lewis. December 28, 1841.

Martin Van Buren

"Banks properly established and conducted are highly useful to the business of the country, and will doubtless continue to exist in the States so long as they conform to their laws and are found to be safe and beneficial."
  —Letter in the Ford Collection. Dated 1842.

Rutherford Hayes

"I am less disposed to think of a West Point education as requisite for business than I was at first. Good sense and energy are the qualities required."
   —Remark to Uncle Sardis. Civil War Era.[1]

"The bold enterprises are the successful ones. Take counsel of hopes rather than of fears to win in this business."
   —Diary. December, 16 1861.

Woodrow Wilson

"Business underlies everything in our national life, including our spiritual life. Witness the fact that in the Lord's Prayer, the first petition is for daily bread. No one can worship God or love his neighbor on an empty stomach."
   —Speech in New York. May 23, 1912.

Calvin Coolidge

"The chief business of the American people is business."
   —Speech to the American Society of Newspaper Editors.
      January 17, 1925.

Herbert Hoover

"It is just as important that business keep out of government as that government keep out of business."
   —Address on the 150th Anniversary of the Battle of Kings
      Mountain. October 7, 1930.[2]

"Let me remind you that credit is the lifeblood of business, the lifeblood of prices and jobs."
   —Address at the Coliseum in Des Moines, Iowa.
      October 4, 1932.

Franklin Roosevelt

"Prosperous farmers mean more employment, more prosperity for the workers and the business men of every industrial area in the whole country."
— Campaign Address at Boston, Massachusetts.
October 30, 1940.

John Kennedy

"My father always told me that all businessmen were sons of bitches, but I never believed it till now."
— Statement to Advisors. *The New York Times.* April 23, 1962.

Ronald Reagan

"The best minds are not in government. If any were, business would steal them away."
— Joking statement on *InformationWeek* (1998).[3]

"Government is the people's business and every man, woman and child becomes a shareholder with the first penny of tax paid."
— Remarks at the New York City Partnership Luncheon in New York. January 14, 1982.

George W. Bush

"I understand small business growth. I was one."
— Speech at "Celebration of Reading" Event. April 26, 2001.

"We believe ranchers and farmers and family business owners can make better decisions about the future than the government can."
— Remarks on the Office of Management and Budget Mid-Session Review. July 11, 2007.

Barack Obama

"That is the true genius of America, a faith in the simple dreams of its people, the insistence on small miracles. That we can say what we think; write what we think, without hearing a sudden knock on the door. That we can have an idea and start our own business without paying a bribe or hearing a sudden knock on the door."

—Speech at the Democratic National Convention. July 27, 2004.

1   Thomas Harry Williams, *Hayes of the Twenty-Third: the Civil War Volunteer Officer* (1994), pg. 93.
2   Hoover has been noted saying this quote at several occasions, verbatim or paraphrased.
3   Issues 684-689.

CHAPTER FOUR

Change

Thomas Jefferson

"Nothing is unchangeable but the inherent and unalienable rights of man."
—Remark to John Cartwright. June 5, 1824.

"It behooves every man who values liberty for himself, to resist invasions of it in the case of others, or their case may, by change of circumstances, become his own."
—Letter to Dr. Benjamin Rush. April 21, 1808.

Martin Van Buren

"Those who have wrought great changes in the world never succeeded by gaining over chiefs; but always by exciting the multitude. The first is the resource of intrigue and produces only secondary results; the second is the resort of genius and transforms the universe."
—*The New Monthly*. January 1823.[1]

Millard Fillmore

"It is not strange to mistake change for progress."
—Third Annual Message December 6, 1852.

Benjamin Harrison

"I knew that my staying up would not change the election result if I were defeated, while if elected I had a hard day ahead of me. So I thought a night's rest was best in any event."
—Quoted by Bryan Curtis in *A Call to America: Inspiring and Empowering Quotations from the 43 Presidents of the United States* (2002).

Woodrow Wilson

"A conservative is someone who makes no changes and consults his grandmother when in doubt."
—Attributed by Raymond B. Fosdick in *Report of the Woodrow Wilson Foundation* (1963).[2]

"If you want to make enemies, try to change something."
—Address at World's Salesmanship Congress, Detroit. July, 10 1916.

Herbert Hoover

"The slogan of progress is changing from the full dinner pail to the full garage."
—Campaign Speech in New York. October 22, 1928.

Franklin Roosevelt

"Favor comes because for a brief moment in the great space of human change and progress some general human purpose finds in him a satisfactory embodiment."
—Final Pre-Presidential Speech. November 7, 1932.

Harry Truman

"Men make history and not the other way around. In periods where there is no leadership, society stands still. Progress occurs when courageous, skillful leaders seize the opportunity to change things for the better."
—Quoted by Gregory Morris, *In Pursuit of Leadership* (2006).[3]

John Kennedy

"Change is the law of life. And those who look only to the past or present are certain to miss the future."
—Address in the Assembly Hall at the Paulskirche in Frankfurt. June 25, 1963.

Richard Nixon

"Any change is resisted because bureaucrats have a vested interest in the chaos in which they exist."
—Statement to Peter Flannigan in 1969.

"In the long term we can hope that religion will change the nature of man and reduce conflict."
—*In Real Peace: No more Vietnams* (1990).

"I don't think that a leader can control, to any great extent, his destiny. Very seldom can he step in and change the situation if the forces of history are running in another direction."
—In *The Kiwanis Magazine* (1968).[4]

Jimmy Carter

"We must adjust to changing times and still hold to unchanging principles."
—Inaugural Address. January 20, 1977.

Ronald Reagan

"All great change in America begins at the dinner table."
—Farewell Address to the Nation. January 11, 1989.

Bill Clinton

"I don't believe you can find any evidence of the fact that I have changed government policy solely because of a contribution."
—The President's News Conference. March 7, 1997.

George W. Bush

"Therapy isn't going to cause terrorists to change their mind."
—*The Washington Times*. June 18, 2009.

Barack Obama

"Change will not come if we wait for some other person or some other time."
—Super Tuesday Primaries Speech in Chicago, Illinois. February 5, 2008.

"We are the ones we've been waiting for. We are the change that we seek."
—Super Tuesday Primaries Speech in Chicago, Illinois. February 5, 2008.

1   Vol. 5 pg. 288. *The New Monthly*. January 1823.
2   Pg. 49.
3   *In Pursuit of Leadership* (2006) by Gregory Morris, Pg. 21.
4   Vol. 53. *The Kiwanis* Magazine (1968).

CHAPTER FIVE

Constitution

George Washington

"The Constitution is the guide which I never will abandon."
  —Statement to the Boston Selectmen, Mount Vernon.
    July 28, 1795.

"The Constitution vests the power of declaring war in Congress."
  —Letter to William Moultrie. August 28, 1793.

"The basis of our political system is the right of the people to make and to alter their constitutions of government."
  —Farewell Address. September 19, 1796.

John Adams

"All the perplexities, confusion and distress in America arise, not from defects in their Constitution or Confederation, not from want of honor or virtue, so much as from the downright ignorance of the nature of coin, credit and circulation."
  —Letter to Thomas Jefferson. August 23, 1787.

"Our Constitution was made only for a moral and religious people. It is wholly inadequate to the government of any other."
 —Letter to the Officers of the First Brigade of the Third Division of the Militia of Massachusetts. October 11, 1798.

Thomas Jefferson

"The constitutions of most of our States assert that all power is inherent in the people."
 —Letter to John Cartwright (1824).

James Madison

"The Constitution preserves the advantage of being armed which Americans possess over the people of almost every other nation where the governments are afraid to trust the people with arms."
 —*The Federalist*. January 29, 1788.[1]

"The people are the only legitimate fountain of power, and it is from them that the constitutional charter is derived."
 —*The Federalist*. February 2, 1788.

"Do not separate text from historical background. If you do, you will have perverted and subverted the Constitution, which can only end in a distorted, bastardized form of illegitimate government."
 —*The Federalist*. January 19, 1788.[2]

"The happy Union of these States is a wonder; their Constitution a miracle; their example the hope of Liberty throughout the world."
 —Letter to Samuel Kercheval. September 7, 1829.

Andrew Jackson

"All the rights secured to the citizens under the Constitution are worth nothing, except guaranteed to them by an independent and virtuous Judiciary."
  —Statement Shortly after Leaving Post of Florida's Military Governorship (1822).[3]

"The Constitution and the laws are supreme and the Union indissoluble."
  —Message to Congress. January 16, 1833.

James Polk

"One great object of the Constitution was to restrain majorities from oppressing minorities or encroaching upon their just rights."
  —Inaugural Address. March 4, 1845.

Zachary Taylor

"In the discharge of duties my guide will be the Constitution, which I this day swear to preserve, protect, and defend."
  —Inaugural Address. March 5, 1849.

Franklin Pierce

"Even here in the loyal States, the mailed hand of military usurpation strikes down the liberties of the people, and its foot tramples on a desecrated Constitution."
  —Speech in Concord, New Hampshire. July 4, 1863.

"The storm of frenzy and faction must inevitably dash itself in vain against the unshaken rock of the Constitution."
  —Third Annual Message. December 31, 1855.

James Buchanan

"The great constitutional corrective in the hands of the people against usurpation of power, or corruption by their agents is the right of suffrage; and this when used with calmness and deliberation will prove strong enough."
—Letter to General Jackson. May 29, 1825.

"There is nothing stable but Heaven and the Constitution."
—Statement. May 13, 1856.

Abraham Lincoln

"Don't interfere with anything in the Constitution. That must be maintained, for it is the only safeguard of our liberties."
—Speech at Kalamazoo, Michigan. August 27, 1856.

"We the people are the rightful masters of both Congress and the courts, not to overthrow the Constitution but to overthrow the men who pervert the Constitution."
—Speech in Cincinnati, Ohio. September 15, 1859.

Andrew Johnson

"Honest conviction is my courage; the Constitution is my guide."
—Speech at White House. February 22, 1866.

"Outside of the Constitution we have no legal authority more than private citizens, and within it we have only so much as that instrument gives us. This broad principle limits all our functions and applies to all subjects."
—Speech to House of Representatives. March 2, 1867.

"I am sworn to uphold the Constitution as Andy Johnson understands it and interprets it."
—Impeachment Trial. March 5-26, 1868.

Calvin Coolidge

"To live under the American Constitution is the greatest political privilege that was ever accorded to the human race."
　　—Address at the White House. December 12, 1924.

Franklin Roosevelt

"The United States Constitution has proved itself the most marvelously elastic compilation of rules of government ever written."
　　—*New York Times.* March 3, 1930.

Lyndon Johnson

"It is the genius of our Constitution that under its shelter of enduring institutions and rooted principles there is ample room for the rich fertility of American political invention."
　　—Annual Message to the Congress on the State of the
　　　　Union. January 12, 1966.

Gerald Ford

"Our constitution works. Our great republic is a government of laws, not of men."
　　—First Presidential Speech to the Nation following
　　　　Resignation of Richard Nixon. August 9, 1974.

"Benjamin Franklin, addressing himself to religious faith and worship in God in the society in which he lived, told the framers of the Constitution: "Without [God's] concurring aid, we shall succeed in this political building no better than the builders of Babel. We shall be divided by our little partial local interests. Our projects will be confounded and we ourselves shall become a reproach and a by-word down to future ages."
　　—Comments during the National Prayer Breakfast,
　　　　Washington Hilton Hotel. January 29, 1976.

Jimmy Carter

The Constitution audaciously proposed a new plan of government—a government through which the new Nation's people could, in the words of the Preamble, "form a more perfect Union, establish Justice, insure domestic Tranquility, provide for the common defense, promote the general Welfare, and secure the Blessings of Liberty to ourselves and our Posterity . . ."
  —Proclamation 4517: Citizenship Day and Constitution
      Week. August 29, 1977.

"With amendments, notably the Bill of Rights, that Constitution has endured these 190 years as the supreme law of our land. We are its inheritors—the "posterity" whose liberty the Founding Fathers wished to secure—and it is fitting for us to mark the anniversary of what they did."
  —Proclamation 4517: Citizenship Day and Constitution
      Week. 1977 August 29, 1977.

Ronald Reagan

"The Constitution protects the right to human life."
  —The President's News Conference. March 6, 1981.

"The people make the Constitution, and the people can unmake it. It is the creature of their own will, and lives only by their will."
  —Proclamation 4949: Citizenship Day and Constitution
      Week. June 24, 1982.

"Almost all the world's constitutions are documents in which governments tell the people what their privileges are. Our Constitution is a document in which "We the People" tell the government what *it* is allowed to do."
  —Farewell Address to the Nation. January 11, 1989.

George H. W. Bush

"Not every American can recite the Constitution. But most of us can feel it. We feel it because Americans, through their daily deeds, give real life to American principles."
— Address to the Nation on the Supreme Court Nomination of Clarence Thomas. September 6, 1991.

"For more than two centuries our national soul, the U.S. Constitution, has given life to the values of equality before the law. While people try from time to time to bury that spirit beneath an avalanche of lawsuits, technicalities and decrees, every American knows that profound notions of fairness, justice, equality, and civility define us and bind us."
— Address to the Nation on the Supreme Court Nomination of Clarence Thomas. September 6, 1991.

Bill Clinton

"We don't need a constitutional amendment; we need action."
— Address before a Joint Session of the Congress on the State of the Union. February 4, 1997.

"You know, when the Framers finished crafting our Constitution in Philadelphia, Benjamin Franklin stood in Independence Hall, and he reflected on the carving of the Sun that was on the back of a chair he saw. The Sun was low on the horizon. So he said this—he said, "I've often wondered whether that Sun was rising or setting. Today," Franklin said, "I have the happiness to know it's a rising Sun." Today, because each succeeding generation of Americans has kept the fire of freedom burning brightly, lighting those frontiers of possibility; we all still bask in the glow and the warmth of Mr. Franklin's rising Sun. After 224 years, the American Revolution continues. We remain a new nation. And as long as our dreams outweigh our memories, America will be

forever young. That is our destiny. And this is our moment."
—Address before a Joint Session of the Congress on the
State of the Union. January 27, 2000.

George W. Bush

"We celebrate the durable wisdom of our Constitution and
recall the deep commitments that unite our country."
—Inaugural Address. January 20, 2005.

"I pledged to honor our Constitution and laws, and I asked you
to join me in setting a tone of civility and respect in
Washington."
—Speech before a Joint Session of the Congress on
Administration Goals. February 27, 2001.

Barack Obama

"We find unity in our incredible diversity, drawing on the promise enshrined in our Constitution: The notion that we're all created equal; that no matter who you are or what you look like, if
you abide by the law, you should be protected by it; if you adhere
to our common values, you should be treated no different than
anyone else."
—Address before a Joint Session of the Congress on the
State of the Union. January 27, 2010.

"We amended our Constitution to extend the democratic principles that we hold dear. And I stand before you today as
President of the most powerful nation on Earth, but recognizing
that once, the color of my skin would have denied me the right
to vote."
—Speech at the University of Yangon in Rangoon, Burma.
November 19, 2012.

"Our Constitution protects the right to practice free speech."
—Remarks to the United Nations General Assembly in New York City. September 25, 2012.

"We may have differences in policy, but we all believe in the rights enshrined in our Constitution: We may have different opinions, but we believe in the same promise that says this is a place where you can make it if you try. We may have different backgrounds, but we believe in the same dream that says this is a country where anything is possible, no matter who you are, no matter where you come from."
—Address before a Joint Session of the Congress on the State of the Union. January 25, 2011.

---

1   No. 46.
2   No. 41.
3   See: *Journal and Proceedings of the North Carolina State Bar Annual Meeting* (1938), North Carolina State Bar.

CHAPTER SIX

Country

George Washington

"I have no other view than to promote the public good, and am unambitious of honors not founded in the approbation of my Country."
—Letter to Henry Laurens. January 31, 1778.

"The country has a right to concentrate your affections."
—Farewell Address. September 19, 1796.

"Every post is honorable in which a man can serve his country."
—Letter to Benedict Arnold. September 14, 1775.

John Adams

"My country has contrived for me the most insignificant office that ever the invention of man contrived or his imagination conceived."
—Letter to Mrs. Adams. December 19, 1793.

Thomas Jefferson

"The spirit of this country is totally adverse to a large military force."
—Letter to Chandler Price. February 28, 1807.

"Our country is now taking so steady a course as to show by what road it will pass to destruction, to wit: by consolidation of power first, and then corruption, it's necessary consequence."
—Letter to Nathaniel Macon. October 20, 1821.

"If God is just, I tremble for my country."
—In His *Notes on Virginia* (1782).

"In every country and every age, the priest had been hostile to Liberty."
—Letter to Horatio Spafford. March 17, 1814.

James Madison

"A well-regulated militia, composed of the body of the people, trained in arms, is the best most natural defense of a free country."
—Second Amendment to the United States Constitution. December 15, 1791.

"Let me recommend the best medicine in the world: a long journey, at a mild season, through a pleasant country, in easy stages."
—Letter to Horatio Gates. February 23, 1794.

James Monroe

"Our country may be likened to a new house. We lack many things, but we possess the most precious of all—liberty!"
—In *American Anecdotes* (1830).

Andrew Jackson

"I weep for the liberty of my country when I see at this early day of its successful experiment that corruption has been imputed to many members of the House of Representatives, and the rights of the people have been bartered for promises of office."
—Letter to John Coffee. February 19, 1825.

"Every good citizen makes his country's honor his own, and cherishes it not only as precious but as sacred. He is willing to risk his life in its defense and it's conscious that he gains protection while he gives it."
—Speech. Recorded by C. Bronson (1845).

"The brave man inattentive to his duty is worth little more to his country than the coward who deserts in the hour of danger."
—Address to Troops in Mississippi. January 8, 1815.

Martin Van Buren

"Our country presents on every side the evidences of that continued favor under whose auspices it, has gradually risen from a few feeble and dependent colonies to a prosperous and powerful confederacy."
—First Annual Message. December 5, 1837.

"There is a power in public opinion in this country—and I thank God for it."
—Speech at the U.S. Senate. December 5, 1837.

James Polk

"Peace, plenty, and contentment reign throughout our borders, and our beloved country presents a sublime moral spectacle to the world."
—Fourth Annual Message. December 5, 1848.

"May the boldest fear and the wisest tremble when incurring responsibilities on which may depend our country's peace and prosperity, and in some degree the hopes and happiness of the whole human family."
—Inaugural Address. March 4, 1845.

Zachary Taylor

"I have no private purpose to accomplish, no party objectives to build up, no enemies to punish—nothing to serve but my country."
—Letter to Capt. J.S. Allison. April 22nd, 1848.

Millard Fillmore

"The man who can look upon a crisis without being willing to offer himself upon the altar of his country is not fit for public trust."
—Speech in Louisville, Kentucky. March 15, 1854.

"May God save the country, for it is evident that the people will not."
—Letter to Henry Clay. November 11, 1844.

"The whole country is full of enterprise."
—Third Annual Message. December 6, 1852.

James Buchanan

"Whatever the result may be, I shall carry to my grave the consciousness that I at least meant well for my country."
—Speech to Congress. January 8, 1861.

"Public opinion in this country is all-powerful."
—Third Annual Message to Congress on the State of the Union. December 19, 1859.

Abraham Lincoln

"I hope to stand firm enough to not go backward, and yet not go forward fast enough to wreck the country's cause."
—Letter to Zachariah Chandler. November 20, 1863.

"Public opinion in this country is everything."
—Speech in Columbus, Ohio. September 16, 1859.

"This country belongs to the people who inhabit it. Whenever they shall grow weary of the existing government, they can exercise their constitutional right of amending it, or exercise their revolutionary right to overthrow it."
—First Inaugural Address. March 4, 1861.

Andrew Johnson

"Friendship between two countries must rest on the basis of mutual justice."
—First Annual Message. December 4, 1865.

Rutherford Hayes

"He serves his party best who serves his country best."
—Inaugural Address. March 5, 1877.

James Garfield

"Whoever controls the volume of money in any country is absolute master of all industry and commerce."
—Reported in *Money*. March 1899.[2]

Grover Cleveland

"Let us constantly bear in mind that our country is something which, as an example and interpreter of freedom, belongs to the

world, and which, in its blessed mission, belongs to humanity."
—Address at the Jewelers' Association Annual Dinner,
New York. November 21, 1890.

Theodore Roosevelt

"A man who is good enough to shed his blood for the country is good enough to be given a square deal afterwards."
—In His *A Square Deal* (1906).[3]

"Every immigrant who comes here should be required within five years to learn English or leave the country."
—Statement to Kansas City Star. April 27, 1918.

"The pacifist is as surely a traitor to his country and to humanity as is the most brutal wrongdoer."
—Speech in Pittsburg, Pennsylvania. July 27, 1917.

"We can have no "50-50" allegiance in this country. Either a man is an American and nothing else, or he is not an American at all."
—Speech in Pittsburg, Pennsylvania. July 27, 1917.

William Taft

"The welfare of the farmer is vital to that of the whole country."
—Address in Hot Springs, Virginia. August 8, 1908.

Woodrow Wilson

"If there are men in this country big enough to own the government of the United States, they are going to own it."
—In his *The New Freedom* (1913).

"Princeton is no longer a thing for Princeton men to please themselves with. Princeton is a thing with which Princeton men

must satisfy the country."
   —Address before the University Club of Chicago.
      May 12, 1910.

Calvin Coolidge

"Patriotism is easy to understand in America. It means looking out for yourself by looking out for your country."
   —Memorial Day Speech in Northampton, Massachusetts.
      May 30, 1923.

Franklin Roosevelt

"Prosperous farmers mean more employment, more prosperity for the workers and the business men of every industrial area in the whole country."
   —Campaign Address at Boston, Massachusetts.
      October 30, 1940.

"We are going to make a country in which no one is left out."
   —Campaign Speech, as noted by Roosevelt's Secretary of
      Labor Frances Perkins (1930s).

"The ultimate rulers of our democracy are not a President and senators and congressmen and government officials, but the voters of this country."
   —Address at Marietta, Ohio. July 8, 1938.

Harry Truman

"We should all get together and make a country in which everybody can eat turkey whenever he pleases."
   —*Life*. Jan 30, 1956.[4]

Dwight Eisenhower

"The purpose is clear. It is safety with solvency. The country is

entitled to both."
—Address to the American Society of Newspaper Editors
and the International Press Institute. April 17, 1958.

John Kennedy

"And so, my fellow Americans, ask not what your country can do for you; ask what you can do for your country."
—Inaugural Address. January 20, 1961.

"I look forward to a great future for America—a future in which our country will match its military strength with our moral restraint, its wealth with our wisdom, its power with our purpose."
—Remarks at Amherst College upon Receiving an
Honorary Degree. October 26, 1963.

Lyndon Johnson

"The moon and other celestial bodies should be free for exploration and use by all countries. No country should be permitted to advance a claim of sovereignty."
—Statement by the President on the Need for a Treaty
Governing Exploration of Celestial Bodies. May 7, 1966.

"I report to you that our country is challenged at home and abroad."
—State of the Union Address. January 17, 1968.

Ronald Reagan

"It's difficult to believe that people are still starving in this country because food isn't available."
—The President's News Conference. June 11, 1986.

"If we love our country, we should also love our countrymen."
—Inaugural Address. January 20, 1981.

George H. W. Bush

"Leadership to me means duty, honor, and country."
    —Quoted by Bryan Curtis in *A Call to America* (2002).

Bill Clinton

"Let us all take more responsibility, not only for ourselves and our families but for our communities and our country."
    —Inaugural Address. January 20, 1993.

George W. Bush

"I know it's going to be the private sector that leads this country out of the current economic times we're in. You can spend your money better than the government can."
    —Speech in Erie, Pennsylvania. June 17, 2009.

Barack Obama

"I know my country has not perfected itself."
    —Speech in Berlin, Germany. July 24, 2008.

1   Section XII.
2   Vol. 2, No. 9. *Money*. March 1899.
3   Pg. 133.
4   Vol. 40, No. 5. *Life*. January 1956.

CHAPTER SEVEN

Democracy

George Washington

"Democratically, States must always feel before they can see: it is this that makes their Governments slow, but the people will be right at last."
—Letter to Marquis de Lafayette. July 25, 1785.

John Adams

"Remember, democracy never lasts long. It soon wastes, exhausts, and murders itself."

"There never was a democracy yet that did not commit suicide."

"Democracy while it lasts is more bloody than either aristocracy or monarchy."
—In a Collection of Letters to John Taylor dated April 15, 1814-April 8, 1824.

Thomas Jefferson

"A democracy is nothing more than mob rule, where fifty-one

percent of the people may take away the rights of the other forty-nine."
—Manuscript (1813).[1]

James Madison

"A pure democracy is a society consisting of a small number of citizens, who assemble and administer the government in person."
—*The Federalist.* November 22, 1787.[2]

Andrew Jackson

"Democracy shows not only its power in reforming governments, but in regenerating a race of men and this is the greatest blessing of free governments."
—Letter to James Hamilton, Jr. June 29, 1828.

Franklin Pierce

"There is the effective democracy of the nation and there is the vital essence of its being and its greatness."
—First Annual Message, Washington D.C.
December 5, 1853.

James Buchanan

"The generations of mortals, one after the other, rise and sink and are forgotten; but the principles of Democracy, which we have inherited from our revolutionary fathers, will endure to bless mankind throughout all generations."
—Speech at the Mass Meeting of the Democracy of
Western Pennsylvania, Greensburg. October 7, 1852.[3]

"I like the noise of Democracy!"
—Speech at the Mass Meeting of the Democracy of
Western Pennsylvania, Greensburg. October 7, 1852.

Abraham Lincoln

"As I would not be a slave, so I would not be a master. This expresses my idea of democracy."
—Statement to Mary Todd Lincoln, in *Collected Works* (1858).[4]

"Democracy is the government of the people, by the people, for the people."
—Gettysburg Address. November 19, 1863

Grover Cleveland

"The ship of democracy, which has weathered all storms, may sink through the mutiny of those on board."
—Letter to Wilson S. Bissell. February 15, 1894.

"In each succeeding year it more clearly appears that our democratic principle needs no apology."
—First Inaugural Address. March 4, 1885.

Woodrow Wilson

"Democracy is not so much a form of government as a set of principles."
—*Atlantic Monthly*. Boston, Massachusetts. March 1901.

"That a peasant may become king does not render the kingdom democratic."
—Speech in Chattanooga, Tennessee. August 31, 1910.

"The world must be made safe for democracy. Its peace must be planted upon the tested foundations of political liberty."
—Address to Congress for a Declaration of War Against Germany. April 2, 1917.

Warren Harding

"There is something inherently wrong, something out of accord with the ideals of representative democracy, when one portion of our citizenship turns its activities to private gain amid defensive war while another is fighting, sacrificing, or dying for national preservation."
  —Inaugural Address. March 4, 1921.

Calvin Coolidge

"There is no force so democratic as the force of an ideal."
  —Speech in New York City. November 27, 1920.

Franklin Roosevelt

"The ultimate rulers of our democracy are not a President and senators and congressmen and government officials, but the voters of this country."
  —Address at Marietta, Ohio. July 8, 1938.

"Democracy cannot succeed unless those who express their choice are prepared to choose wisely."
  —Message for American Education Week. September 27, 1938

"The real safeguard of democracy is education."
  —Message for American Education Week. September 27, 1938

"No system of government gives so much to the individual or exacts so much as a democracy."
  —Message for American Education Week. September 27, 1938

John Kennedy

"The ignorance of one voter in a democracy impairs the security of all."
  —Remark at the 90th Anniversary Convocation of
    Vanderbilt University, Nashville, Tennessee. May 18, 1963.

Gerald Ford

"Our values, our principles, and our determination to succeed as a free and democratic people will give us a torch to light the way."
  —Address to the State Conference of the Order of
    DeMolay, Grand Rapids, Michigan. September 7, 1968

Jimmy Carter

"The best way to enhance freedom in other lands is to demonstrate here that our democratic system is worthy of emulation."
  —Inaugural Address. January 20, 1977.

"The experience of democracy is like the experience of life itself-always changing, infinite in its variety, sometimes turbulent and all the more valuable for having been tested by adversity."
  —Speech to Parliament of India. June 2, 1978.

"We always believed that we were part of a great movement of humanity itself called democracy."
  —In Televised Speech. July 15, 1979.

Ronald Reagan

"Democracy is worth dying for, because it's the most deeply honorable form of government ever devised by man."
  —Remark at a ceremony commemorating the 40th
    anniversary of the Normandy Invasion, D-Day. June 6,
    1984.

"Without God, democracy will not and cannot long endure."
   —Remark at an Ecumenical Prayer Breakfast, Dallas, Texas.
     August 23, 1984.

"Our armies are here for only one purpose—to protect and defend democracy."
   —Remark at a Ceremony Commemorating the 40th
     Anniversary of the Normandy Invasion, D-Day.
     June 6, 1984.

"Only those humble enough to admit they're sinners can bring to democracy the tolerance it requires in order to survive."
   —Remark at an Ecumenical Prayer Breakfast, Dallas, Texas.
     August 23, 1984.

George H. W. Bush

"We love your adherence to democratic principles and to the democratic process."
   —Toast to Ferdinand Marcos. June 30, 1981.

Bill Clinton

"Democracies don't go to war against each other."
   —Speech at Georgetown University, Washington D.C.
     December 12, 1991.

"Democracies don't attack each other."
   —State of the Union Address. January 25, 1994.

"Democratic countries make better neighbors. They don't repress their people. They trade on the open market."
   —Press Briefing by Dee Dee Myers. September 15, 1994.

George W. Bush

"Our aim is a democratic peace—a peace founded upon the dignity and rights of every man and woman."
   —Address before a Joint Session of the Congress on the State of the Union. January 20, 2004.

"President Washington believed that the success of our democracy would also depend on the virtue of our citizens."
   —On a visit to Mount Vernon to Honor President Washington's 275th Birthday. February 19, 2007.

"Lasting peace is gained as justice and democracy advance."
   —Remark on U.S.-British Relations and Foreign Policy at Whitehall Palace, London. November 19, 2003.

Barack Obama

"'We the people, in order to form a more perfect union.' Two hundred and twenty one years ago, in a hall that still stands across the street, a group of men gathered and, with these simple words, launched America's improbable experiment in democracy."
   —Speech on Race Relations at the National Constitution Center, Philadelphia, Pennsylvania. March 18 2008.

"The practice of listening to opposing views is essential for effective citizenship. It is essential for our democracy."
   —Commencement Address, University of Michigan in Ann Arbor, Michigan. May 1, 2010.

"The democracy designed by Jefferson and the other Founders was never intended to solve every problem."
   —Commencement Address, University of Michigan in Ann Arbor, Michigan. May 1, 2010.

"The strongest democracies flourish from frequent and lively debate, but they endure when people of every background and belief find a way to set aside smaller differences in service of a greater purpose."
 —First Presidential Press Conference. February 9, 2009.

"The Question for your generation is this: How will you keep our democracy going?"
 —Commencement Address, University of Michigan in Ann Arbor, Michigan. May 1, 2010.

---

1   No. 10.
2   Scholars disagree as to whether this statement was penned originally by Jefferson. Nevertheless, it embodies the underlying philosophy of his "Jeffersonian Democracy," as illustrated in *The Jeffersonian Cyclopedia*.
3   Whether this particular quote was delivered at this particular Mass Meeting is questionable. However, it does accurately express the sentiment of the said event. October 7, 1852.
4   2:532. Quote's authenticity reaffirmed by President Franklin Roosevelt during his visit to Abraham Lincoln's birthplace on June 24, 1936. *Collected Works*. 1858.

CHAPTER EIGHT

Economy

Andrew Jackson

"I cannot too strongly urge the necessity of a rigid economy."
—Fifth Annual Message. December 3, 1833.

John Tyler

"The gloomy picture which our financial department now presents calls for the exercise of a rigid economy in public expenditures and the rendering available of all means within the control of the Government."
—Veto Message. August 9, 1842.

Franklin Pierce

"Administer government with vigilant integrity and rigid economy."
—Second Annual Message. December 4, 1854.

Andrew Johnson

"A sparing economy is itself a great national source."
—First Annual Message. December 4, 1865.

Calvin Coolidge

"Economy is the method by which we prepare today to afford the improvements of tomorrow."
>—Third Annual Message. December 8, 1925.

Herbert Hoover

"Once upon a time my political opponents honored me as possessing the fabulous intellectual and economic power by which I created a worldwide depression all by myself."
>—In *Financial World* (1958).[1]

"With impressive proof on all sides of magnificent progress, no one can rightly deny the fundamental correctness of our economic system."
>—Presidential Nomination Address. August 11, 1928.

"America—a great social and economic experiment, noble in motive and far-reaching in purpose."
>—Letter to Senator William Borah. February 28, 1928.

"Economic depression cannot be cured by legislative action or executive pronouncement. Economic wounds must be healed by the action of the cells of the economic body—the producers and consumers themselves."
>—Statement to Congress. December 2, 1930.

Franklin Roosevelt

"The school is the last expenditure upon which America should be willing to economize."
>—Campaign Address at Kansas City, Missouri. October 13, 1936.

"We must lay hold of the fact that economic laws are not made by nature. They are made by human beings."
—Acceptance Speech in Chicago. July 2, 1932.

"In our personal ambitions we are individualists. But in our seeking for economic and political progress as a nation, we all go up or else all go down as one people."
—Second Inaugural Address. January 20, 1937.

"True individual freedom cannot exist without economic security and independence."
—State of the Union Message to Congress. January 11, 1944.

"But while they prate of economic laws, men and women are starving."
—Address Accepting the Presidential Nomination at the Democratic National Convention in Chicago. July 2, 1932.

"Not only our future economic soundness but the very soundness of our democratic institutions depends on the determination of our government to give employment to idle men."
—Fireside Chat. April 14, 1938.

Harry Truman

"Experience has shown how deeply the seeds of war are planted by economic rivalry and social injustice."
—Address in San Francisco at the Closing Session of the United Nations Conference. June 26, 1945.

John Kennedy

"Geography has made us neighbors. History has made us friends. Economics has made us partners."
—Address before the Canadian Parliament in Ottawa. May 17, 1961.

"The tax on capital gains directly affects the strength and potential for growth in the economy."
— Special Message to the Congress on Tax Reduction and Reform. January 24, 1963.

Lyndon Johnson

"Did you ever think that making a speech on economics is a lot like pissing down your leg? It seems hot to you, but it never does to anyone else."
— Comment to economist J. K. Galbraith, in *A Life in Our Times* (1981).

Ronald Reagan

"The government's view of the economy could be summed up in a few short phrases: If it moves, tax it. If it keeps moving, regulate it. And if it stops moving, subsidize it."
— Remarks to State Chair persons of the National White House Conference on Small Business. August 15, 1986.

"Entrepreneurs and their small enterprises are responsible for almost all the economic growth in the United States."
— Address With Students and Faculty at Moscow State University. May 31, 1988.

Bill Clinton

"In the new economy, information, education, and motivation are everything."
— Remarks to a Joint Session of Parliament in New Delhi. March 22, 2000.

" In today's knowledge-based economy, what you earn depends on what you learn."
— Statement on Signing the American Competitiveness in the Twenty-First Century Act and Non-Immigrant Worker Fee Legislation. October 17, 2000.

George W. Bush

"I know it's going to be the private sector that leads this country out of the current economic times we're in. You can spend your money better than the government can."
—Speech in Erie, Pennsylvania. June 17, 2009.

"In terms of the economy, look, I inherited a recession; I am ending on a recession."
—The President's News Conference. January 12, 2009.

Barack Obama

"Tonight, we gather to affirm the greatness of our nation—not because of the height of our skyscrapers, or the power of our military, or the size of our economy. Our pride is based on a very simple premise, summed up in a declaration made over two hundred years ago."
—Speech at the Democratic National Convention. July 24, 2004.

"I will cut taxes—cut taxes—for 95 percent of all working families, because, in an economy like this, the last thing we should do is raise taxes on the middle class."
—Address Accepting the Presidential Nomination at the Democratic National Convention. August 28, 2008.

"With the changing economy, no one has lifetime employment."
—*Daily Southtown.* Feb. 19, 2005.

1   Vol.109. *Financial World* (1958).

CHAPTER NINE

Education

George Washington

"All I am I owe to my mother. I attribute all my success in life to the moral, intellectual and physical education I received from her."
—Cited by George W. Bush in His Proclamation 7674 Mother's Day, 2003. May 7, 2003.

John Adams

"There are two educations. One should teach us how to make a living and the other how to live."[1]
—*Forum.* June 1929.

Thomas Jefferson

"To penetrate and dissipate these clouds of darkness, the general mind must be strengthened by education."
—Letter to Van der Kemp. July 9, 1820.

"The man who reads nothing at all is better educated than the

man who reads nothing but newspapers."
—Remark Regarding the Missouri Compromise of 1820.[2]

"Educate and inform the whole mass of the people: they are the only sure reliance for the preservation of our liberty."
—Letter to James Madison. December 20, 1787.

James Madison

"Whenever a youth is ascertained to possess talents meriting an education which his parents cannot afford, he should be carried forward at the public expense."
—Letter to W. T. Barry. August 4, 1822.

Rutherford Hayes

"Universal suffrage should rest upon universal education. To this end, liberal and permanent provision should be made for the support of free schools by the State governments, and, if need be, supplemented by legitimate aid from national authority."
—Inaugural Address. March 5, 1877.

"I am less disposed to think of a West Point education as requisite for business than I was at first. Good sense and energy are the qualities required."
—Remark to Uncle Sardis Civil War Era.[3]

"With education the needed law follows without effort and, of course, with power to execute itself; indeed, it seems to execute itself."
—Diary. January 23, 1883.

"Law without education is a dead letter."
—Diary. January 23, 1883.

James Garfield

"Next in importance to freedom and justice is popular education, without which neither freedom nor justice can be permanently maintained."
— Letter Accepting the Presidential Nomination.
  July 12, 1880.

Theodore Roosevelt

"A man who has never gone to school may steal from a freight car; but if he has a university education, he may steal the whole railroad."
— Quoted by Marcus Stadelmann in *U.S. Presidents For Dummies* (2011).

"A thorough knowledge of the Bible is worth more than a college education."
— Quoted in *Stepping Stones: The Complete Bible Narratives* (1941).

"To educate a man in mind and not in morals is to educate a menace to society."
— Quoted by Gerald Ford in his Commencement Address at Warner Pacific College in Portland. May 23, 1976.

Woodrow Wilson

"We have not given science too big a place in our education, but we have made a perilous mistake in giving it too great a preponderance in method in every other branch of study."
— *The Forum*. December 1896.

Franklin Roosevelt

"No group and no government can properly prescribe precisely

what should constitute the body of knowledge with which true education is concerned."
    —Address at Temple University upon receiving an
        Honorary Degree. February 22, 1936.

"Democracy cannot succeed unless those who express their choice are prepared to choose wisely. The real safeguard of democracy, therefore, is education."
    —Message for American Education Week. September 27,
        1938.

Harry Truman

"Upon books the collective education of the race depends; they are the sole instruments of registering, perpetuating and transmitting thought."
    —Quoted by Kaplan in *Kaplan SAT Advanced 2009:
        Intensive Prep for Top Students.*[4]

John Kennedy

"It might be said now that I have the best of both worlds. A Harvard education and a Yale degree."
    —Commencement Address at Yale University. June 11, 1962.

"The goal of education is the advancement of knowledge and the dissemination of truth."
    —Speech at Harvard University. June 14, 1956.

"A child mis-educated is a child lost."
    —Quoted by Paul Harwood in *Educating the First Digital
        Generation* (2007).

"Our progress as a nation can be no swifter than our progress in education. The human mind is our fundamental resource."

—Special Message to the Congress on Education. February 20, 1961.

Lyndon Johnson

"Education is a public investment."
—Remarks at the Dedication of the Crossland Vocational Center in Camp Springs, Maryland. April 27, 1967.

"We have entered an age in which education is not just a luxury permitting some men an advantage over others. It has become a necessity without which a person is defenseless in this complex, industrialized society."
—Commencement Speech at Tufts University. June 9, 1963.

Bill Clinton

"We have to empower all through education."
—Address at the National Education Association School Safety Summit in Los Angeles, California. April 8, 1995.

"In the new economy, information, education, and motivation are everything."
—Remarks to a Joint Session of Parliament in New Delhi. March 22, 2000.

"We don't have to cut education to balance the budget."
—Address at the Clinton/Gore '96 Dinner in Los Angeles, California. September 21, 1995.

"Education is the key to whether individuals can live up to their own dreams."
—Remarks at the National Education Association School Safety Summit in Los Angeles, California. April 8, 1995.

"We need to invest more in education. It's the only way we can offer hope to people of a successful life."
  —Remarks at the National Education Association School Safety Summit in Los Angeles, California. April 8, 1995.

George W. Bush

"Determination and spirit are essential to achieving educational success at every level. All Americans should have opportunities to pursue the American dream."
  —Proclamation 7472—National Historically Black Colleges and Universities Week. September 28, 2001.

"Education should prepare children for jobs, and it also should prepare our children for life."
  —Remarks at the White House Conference on Character and Community. June 19, 2002.

Barack Obama

"We have an obligation and a responsibility to be investing in our students and our schools. We must make sure that people who have the grades, the desire and the will, but not the money, can still get the best education possible."
  —*Black Issues in Higher Education*. October 7, 2004.

---

1   Though this statement may have very well symbolized Adams' philosophy of life, they literal quote is most often attributed to American historian and essayist James Truslow Adams in To "BE" or to "DO" in *Forum*, Jun 1929; vol. 81, No. 6.

2   It is disputed whether this particular quote was uttered by Jefferson. However, it clearly complements a similar quote by Jefferson in a letter to John Holmes on April 22, 1820. "I had for a long time ceased to read newspapers, or pay any attention to public affairs."

3   Thomas Harry Williams, *Hayes of the Twenty-Third: the Civil War Volunteer Officer* (1994), pg. 93.

4   Pg. 137. *Kaplan SAT Advanced 2009: Intensive Prep for Top Students.*

CHAPTER TEN

Error

George Washington

"We should not look back unless it is to derive useful lessons from past errors, and for the purpose of profiting by dearly bought experience."
   —Letter to John Armstrong. March 26, 1781.

"There can be no greater error than to expect, or calculate, upon real favors from nation to nation. It is an illusion which experience must cure, which a just pride ought to discard."
   —The Farewell Address. September 1, 1796.

Thomas Jefferson

"Delay is preferable to error."
   —Letter to George Washington. May 16, 1792.

"Errors of opinion may be tolerated where reason is left free to combat it."
   —Inaugural Address. March 4, 1801.

"He who knows nothing is closer to the truth than he whose mind is filled with falsehoods and errors."
—Letter to John Norvell. June 11, 1807.

"Ignorance is preferable to error."
—*In Notes on the State of Virginia* (1782).

"It is error alone which needs the support of government. Truth can stand by itself."
—*In Notes on the State of Virginia* (1782).

James Madison

"The world is indebted for all the triumphs which have been gained by reason and humanity over error and oppression."
—Report on the Virginia Resolutions at the Session of 1799-1800.

Andrew Jackson

"Any man worth his salt will stick up for what he believes right, but it takes a slightly better man to acknowledge instantly and without reservation that he is in error."
—Quoted by Randy Okray in *Crew Resource Management for the Fire Service* (2004).[1]

Ulysses Grant

"My failures have been errors in judgment, not of intent."
—Eighth Annual Message. December 5, 1876.

Herbert Hoover

"The pause between the errors and trials of the day and the hopes of the night."
—Quoted by Daniel Okrent in *Last Call: the Rise and Fall of Prohibition* (2010).[2]

Lyndon Johnson

"Our most tragic error may have been our inability to establish a rapport and a confidence with the press and television with the communication media."
—Statement to Reporter. Quoted by George Christian in *The President Steps Down* (1970).[3]

---

1   Pg. 25. *Crew Resource Management for the Fire Service* (2004). Some scholars argue this quote is actually attributed to General Peyton C. March.
2   Pg. 304. *Last call: the Rise and Fall of Prohibition* (2010).
3   Pg. 188. *The President Steps Down* (1970).

CHAPTER ELEVEN

Freedom

George Washington

"It may be laid down as a primary position, and the basis of our system, that every Citizen who enjoys the protection of a Free Government owes not only a proportion of his property, but even of his personal services to the defense of it."
—Letter to Alexander Hamilton. May 2, 1783.

"If the freedom of speech is taken away then dumb and silent we may be led, like sheep to the slaughter."
—Newburgh Address. 15 March 1783.

"The time is near at hand which must determine whether Americans are to be free men or slaves."
—Address to Continental Army before Battle of Long Island. August 27, 1776.

John Adams

"The essence of a free government consists in an effectual control of rivalries."
—*Discourses on Davila*, no. 13. 1790.

"There is danger from all men. The only maxim of a free government ought to be to trust no man living with power to endanger the public liberty."
—From His *Notes for an Oration at Braintree*. Spring 1772.

"When people talk of the freedom of writing, speaking or thinking I cannot choose but laugh. No such thing ever existed."
—Letter to Thomas Jefferson. July 15, 1817.

Thomas Jefferson

"No government ought to be without censors; and where the press is free no one ever will."
—Letter to George Washington. September 9, 1792.

"Our greatest happiness does not depend on the condition of life in which chance has placed us, but is always the result of a good conscience, good health, occupation, and freedom in all just pursuits."
—*Notes on Virginia* (1782).

"A wise and frugal government, which shall leave men free to regulate their own pursuits of industry and improvement, and shall not take from the mouth of labor the bread it has earned—this is the sum of good government."
—Inaugural Address. March 4, 1801.

"Every citizen should be a soldier. This was the case with the Greeks and Romans, and must be that of every Free State."
—Letter to James Monroe. June 18, 1813.

"If a nation expects to be free, it expects what never was and never will be."
—Letter to Col. Yancey. January 16, 1816.

"Where the press is free and every man able to read, all is safe."
—Letter to Col. Yancey. January 16, 1816.

"For a people who are free, and who mean to remain so, a well-organized and armed militia is their best security."
—Eighth Annual Message. November 8, 1808.

James Madison

"A well-instructed people alone can be permanently a free people."
—Second Annual Message. December 5, 1810.

"A man has a property in his opinions and the free communication of them."
—Paper Entitled "Property." March 29, 1792.

"I believe there are more instances of the abridgement of freedom of the people by gradual and silent encroachments by those in power than by violent and sudden usurpations."
—Speech at the Virginia Convention to ratify the Federal Constitution. June 6, 1788.

"Learned Institutions ought to be favorite objects with every free people."
—Letter to W. T. Barry. August 4, 1822.

"No nation could preserve its freedom in the midst of continual warfare."
—*Political Observations*. April 20, 1795.

John Q. Adams

"Posterity: you will never know how much it has cost my generation to preserve your freedom. I hope you will make good use of it."
—As Referenced by U.S. Congress, *Congressional Record* March 9, 1999.

Andrew Jackson

"Democracy shows not only its power in reforming governments, but in regenerating a race of men and this is the greatest blessing of free governments."
—Letter to James Hamilton, Jr. June 29, 1828.

William Harrison

"I contend that the strongest of all governments is that which is most free."
—Letter to Bolivar. September 7, 1829.

John Tyler

"Let it be henceforth proclaimed to the world that man's conscience was created free."
—Funeral Oration on the Death of Thomas Jefferson. July 11, 1826.

Millard Fillmore

"Let us remember that revolutions do not always establish freedom."
—Third Annual. December 6, 1852.

James Buchanan

"The ballot box is the surest arbiter of disputes among free men."
—Fourth Annual Message to Congress on the State of the Union. December 3, 1860.

Abraham Lincoln

"America will never be destroyed from the outside. If we falter

and lose our freedoms, it will be because we destroyed ourselves."
> —Address before the Young Men's Lyceum of Springfield, Illinois. January 27, 1838.[1]

"Those who deny freedom to others deserve it not for themselves."
> —Letter to Henry L. Pierce. April 6, 1859.

James Garfield

"The truth will set you free, but first it will make you miserable."
> —Quoted by Henry Ivey in *Two Sides of the River: A Time to Choose* (2011).[2]

"All free governments are managed by the combined wisdom and folly of the people."
> —Letter to B. A. Hinsdale. April 21, 1880.

"Next in importance to freedom and justice is popular education, without which neither freedom nor justice can be permanently maintained."
> —Letter Accepting the Presidential Nomination. July 12, 1880.

Chester Arthur

"Men may die, but the fabric of our free institutions remains unshaken."
> —Inaugural Address. September 22, 1881.

Benjamin Harrison

"When and under what conditions is the black man to have a free ballot? When is he in fact to have those full civil rights which have so long been his in law?"
> —First Annual Message. December 8, 1889.

William McKinley, Jr.

"The free man cannot be long an ignorant man."
   —Address at the Carnegie Library in Pittsburg,
      Pennsylvania. November 3, 1897.

Theodore Roosevelt

"Freedom from effort in the present merely means that there has been effort stored up in the past."
   —Speech before the Hamilton Club in Chicago, Illinois.
      April 10, 1899.

Woodrow Wilson

"America lives in the heart of every man everywhere who wishes to find a region where he will be free to work out his destiny as he chooses."
   —Campaign Speech, Chicago, Illinois. April 6, 1912.

"I would rather belong to a poor nation that was free than to a rich nation that had ceased to be in love with liberty."
   —Address before the Southern Commercial Congress at
      Mobile, Alabama. October 27, 1913.

Herbert Hoover

"It is a paradox that every dictator has climbed to power on the ladder of free speech."
   —Quoted by Joslyn Pine in *Wit and Wisdom of the
      American Presidents: A Book of Quotations* (2000).[3]

"Immediately on attaining power each dictator has suppressed all free speech except his own."
   —Quoted by Paul Tabori in *Twenty Tremendous Years:
      World War II and After* (1961).[4]

"Freedom is the open window through which pours the sunlight of the human spirit and human dignity."
—Speech in West Branch, Iowa. August 10, 1948.

Franklin Roosevelt

"The truth is found when men are free to pursue it."
—Upon Receiving an Honorary Degree from Temple University, Philadelphia. February 22, 1936.

"True individual freedom cannot exist without economic security and independence."
—State of the Union Message to Congress. January 11, 1944.

Harry Truman

"All men are created free and equal and everyone deserves an even break."
—Rear Platform and Other Informal Remarks in Indiana and Ohio. October 26, 1948.

Dwight Eisenhower

"If you want total security, go to prison. There you're fed, clothed, given medical care and so on. The only thing lacking is freedom."
—Quoted by Susan Beller in *Recipe for Peace Now: Reach Out, Encourage, Connect, Inspire, Progress, Eat* (2009).[5]

"The history of free men is never really written by chance but by choice; their choice!"
—Address in Pittsburgh. October 9, 1956.

"The free world must not prove itself worthy of its own past."
—In *What Eisenhower Thinks* (1952).

"Only our individual faith in freedom can keep us free."
—U.S. Congress, *Congressional Record*. December 5, 2006.

"We seek peace, knowing that peace is the climate of freedom."
—Second Inaugural Address. January 21, 1957.

"History does not long entrust the care of freedom to the weak or the timid."
—Inaugural Address. January 20, 1953.

John Kennedy

"The cost of freedom is always high, but Americans have always paid it."
—Radio and Television Report to the American People on the Soviet Arms Buildup in Cuba. October 22, 1962.

"In the long history of the world, only a few generations have been granted the role of defending freedom in its hour of maximum danger. I do not shrink from this responsibility—I welcome it."
—Inaugural Address. January 20, 1961.

"The best road to progress is freedom's road."
—Special Message to the Congress Requesting Appropriations for the Inter-American Fund for Social Progress and for Reconstruction in Chile. March 14, 1961.

"If a free society cannot help the many who are poor, it cannot save the few who are rich."
—Inaugural Address. January 20, 1961.

"The very word 'secrecy' is repugnant in a free and open society; and we are as a people inherently and historically opposed to

secret societies, to secret oaths, and to secret proceedings."
  —Address before the American Newspaper Publishers
    Association, New York City. April 27, 1961.

"Society must set the artist free to follow his vision wherever it takes him."
  —Upon Receiving Honorary Degree from Amherst
    College. October 26, 1963.

Lyndon Johnson

"Freedom is not enough."
  —*Democratic Digest* (1960).[6]

"The fifth freedom is freedom from ignorance."
  —Special Message to the Congress on Education: *The
    Fifth Freedom*. February 5, 1968.

Jimmy Carter

"The best way to enhance freedom in other lands is to demonstrate here that our democratic system is worthy of emulation."
  —Inaugural Address. January 20, 1977.

Ronald Reagan

"Above all, we must realize that no arsenal, or no weapon in the arsenals of the world, is so formidable as the will and moral courage of free men and women."
  —Inaugural Address. January 20, 1981.

"Freedom is never more than one generation away from extinction. We didn't pass it to our children in the bloodstream. It must be fought for, protected, and handed on for them to do the same."
  —Statement at the Annual Meeting of the Phoenix
    Chamber of Commerce. March 30, 1961.

"Freedom prospers when religion is vibrant and the rule of law under God is acknowledged."
> —Statement at the Annual Convention of the National Association of Evangelicals in Orlando, Florida March 8, 1983.

"Man is not free unless government is limited."
> —Farewell Address to the Nation. January 11, 1989.

"We will always remember. We will always be proud. We will always be prepared, so we will always be free."
> —Remarks to Employees at a Rockwell International Facility in Palmdale, California. October 22, 1984.

" A people free to choose will always choose peace."
> —Address at Moscow State University. May 31, 1988.

"Let us be sure that those who come after will say of us in our time that in our time we did everything that could be done. We finished the race; we kept them free; we kept the faith."
> —Address before a Joint Session of the Congress on the State of the Union. January 25, 1984.

George H. W. Bush

"You can't put democracy and freedom back into a box."
> —Statement to Reporters in Kennebunkport, Maine, on the Attempted Coup in the Soviet Union. August 21, 1991.

Bill Clinton

"Just as war is freedom's cost, disagreement is freedom's privilege."
> —Remark at a Memorial Day ceremony at the Vietnam Veterans Memorial. May 31, 1993.

George W. Bush

"We know that dictators are quick to choose aggression, while free nations strive to resolve differences in peace."
—Speech to United Nations General Assembly. September 21, 2004.

"Everywhere that freedom stirs, let tyrants fear."
—Address to the Nation on Iraq from the U.S.S. Abraham Lincoln. May 1, 2003.

"Free nations are peaceful nations. Free nations don't attack each other. Free nations don't develop weapons of mass destruction."
—Speech at the Midwest Airlines Center in Milwaukee. October 3, 2003.

"Everywhere that freedom arrives, humanity rejoices."
—Address to the Nation on Iraq from the U.S.S. Abraham Lincoln. May 1, 2003.

"I believe that God has planted in every heart the desire to live in freedom."
—Address before a Joint Session of the Congress on the State of the Union. January 20, 2004.

Barack Obama

"Contrary to the claims of some of my critics and some of the editorial pages, I am an ardent believer in the free market."
—Statement to the Business Roundtable. February 24, 2010.

"Today we are engaged in a deadly global struggle for those who would intimidate, torture, and murder people for exercising the most basic freedoms. If we are to win this struggle and spread those freedoms, we must keep our own moral compass pointed in a true direction."
—U.S. Congress, *Congressional Record*. February 3, 2005.

1   Source: *Congressional Record*, May 19, 2005. Whether these exact words were uttered in the Lyceum Speech is debatable; however, it does accurately embody the sentiment of the said event.
2   Pg. 210. *Two Sides of the River: A Time to Choose* (2011).
3   Pg. 50. *Wit and Wisdom of the American Presidents: A Book of Quotations* (2000).
4   Pg. 220. *Twenty Tremendous Years: World War II and After* (1961).
5   Pg. 119. *Recipe for Peace Now: Reach Out, Encourage, Connect, Inspire, Progress, Eat* (2009).
6   Vol.7. Democratic National Committee (U.S.).

CHAPTER TWELVE

Friendship

George Washington

"A slender acquaintance with the world must convince every man that actions, not words, are the true criterion of the attachment of friends."
—Letter to Major-General Sullivan. December 15, 1779.

"I can never think of promoting my convenience at the expense of a friend's interest and inclination."
—In *Moral Maxims* (1787).

John Adams

"Now to what higher object can any Mortal aspire than to befriend the Friendless?" [1]
—Letter to Jonathan Sewall. October 1759.

"No man who ever held the office of President would congratulate a friend on obtaining it."
—Letter to Josiah Quincy III. February 14, 1825.

Thomas Jefferson

"I had rather be shut up in a very modest cottage with my books,

my family and a few old friends, dining on simple bacon, and letting the world roll on as it liked, than to occupy the most splendid post, which any human power can give."
—Letter to Alexander Donald. February 7, 1788.

"I own that I am not a friend to a very energetic government. It is always oppressive."
—Letter to James Madison. December 20, 1787.

"We must meet our duty and convince the world that we are just friends and brave enemies."
—Letter to Andrew Jackson. December 3, 1806.

"Friendship is precious; not only in the shade, but in the sunshine of life, and thanks to a benevolent arrangement the greater part of life is sunshine."
—Letter to Maria Cosway in 1786.

"I never consider a difference of opinion in politics, in religion, or in philosophy, as cause for withdrawing from a friend."
—Letter to William Hamilton. April 22, 1800.

"Peace and friendship with all mankind is our wisest policy, and I wish we may be permitted to pursue it."
—Letter to Mr. Dumas. May 6, 1786.

"Peace, commerce and honest friendship with all nations; entangling alliances with none."
—First Inaugural Address. March 4, 1801.

James Madison

"My dear friend: May heaven favor your cause, and make you the channel through which it may pour its favors."
—Letter to Gilbert du Motier, Marquis de Lafayette.
June 16, 1792.

James Monroe

"It is our duty to cultivate friendly relations and to act with kindness and liberality in all our transactions."
    —Inaugural Address. March 4, 1817.

"Cultivate by a fair and honorable conduct the friendship of all."
    —Inaugural Address. March 4, 1817.

John Q. Adams

"There still remains one effort of magnanimity, one sacrifice of prejudice and passion: It is that of discarding every remnant of rancor against each other, and of embracing as countrymen and friends."
    —Inaugural Address. March 4, 1825.

Andrew Jackson

"It will be my study to preserve peace and to cultivate friendship on fair and honorable terms."
    —Inaugural Address. March 4, 1829.

Martin Van Buren

"We sedulously cultivate the friendship of all nations as the conditions most compatible with our welfare and principles."
    —Inaugural Address. March 4, 1837.

William Harrison

"It is my intention to use every means in my power to preserve friendly intercourse."
    —Inaugural Address. March 4, 1841.

" Always be a friend to your countrymen, never their flatterer."[2]
    —Inaugural Address. March 4, 1841.

John Tyler

"So far as it depends on the course of this government, our relations of good will and friendship will be sedulously cultivated with all nations."
—Special Session Message. June 1, 1841

Zachary Taylor

"It is our true policy to cultivate the most friendly relations."
—Annual Message. December 4, 1849.

Millard Fillmore

"Friendly relations with all, but entangling alliances with none, has long been a maxim with us. Our true mission is not to propagate our opinions or impose upon other countries our form of government by artifice or force, but to teach by example and show by our success, moderation, and justice."
—Second Annual Message. December 2, 1851.

Franklin Pierce

"Cultivate peace and friendship."
—Second Annual Message. December 4, 1854.

"It has been my earnest desire to maintain friendly intercourse."
—First Annual Message. December 5, 1853.

James Buchanan

"In entering upon this great office I must humbly invoke the God of our fathers for wisdom and firmness to execute its high and responsible duties in such a manner as to restore harmony and ancient friendship among the people."
—Inaugural Address. March 4, 1857.

Abraham Lincoln

"The better part of one's life consists of his friendships."
 —Letter to Joseph Gillespie. July 13, 1849.

"We are not enemies, but friends. We must not be enemies. Though passion may have strained, it must not break our bonds of affection."
 —First Inaugural Address. March 4, 1861.

Andrew Johnson

"Friendship between two must rest on the basis of mutual justice."[3]
 —First Annual Message. December 4, 1865.

Ulysses Grant

"The friend in my adversity I shall always cherish most. I can better trust those who helped to relieve the gloom of my dark hours than those who are so ready to enjoy with me the sunshine of my prosperity."
 —Quoted in *Forbes* (1960).[4]

Rutherford Hayes

"As friends go it is less important to live."
 —Diary. July 8, 1887.

Chester Arthur

"Increase friendship between the different sections of the land: for liberty, justice, and constitutional government."
 —Proclamation 254—Thanksgiving Day. October 25, 1882.

Grover Cleveland

"The genius of our institutions, the needs of our people in their

home life, and the attention which is demanded for the settlement and development of the resources of our vast territory, is the policy of Monroe and of Washington and Jefferson—'Peace, commerce, and honest friendship with all nations; entangling alliance with none.'"
   —Inaugural Address. March 4, 1885.

Benjamin Harrison

"Find a higher satisfaction in the evidences of unselfish friendship."
   —First Annual Message. December 3, 1889.

William McKinley, Jr.

"It is important that our relations with people shall be of the most friendly character."
   —Second Annual Message. December 5, 1898.

Theodore Roosevelt

"At last the light was stilled in the kindly eyes and the breath went from the lips that even in mortal agony uttered no words save of forgiveness to his murderer, of love for his friends, and of faltering trust in the will of the Most High."
   —Statement on President McKinley's Death.
      December 3, 1901.

William Taft

"Common interest lies in maintaining the most friendly and cordial relations with each other."
   —Second Annual Message. December 6, 1910.

Woodrow Wilson

"Friendship is genuine and disinterested."
   —Address to a Joint Session of Congress. August 27, 1913.

WarrenHarding

"There is a genuine aspiration in every American breast for a tranquil friendship with all the world."
> —Address Accepting the Republican Presidential
> Nomination. June 12, 1920.

"We crave friendship and harbor no hate."
> —Inaugural Address. March 4, 1921.

Calvin Coolidge

"International friendship is a guarantee of world peace."
> —Proclamation 1680. November 5, 1923.

"International friendship and good will are of very large money value."
> —Speech at the Laying of the Corner Stone of the National
> Press Club Building, Washington, D.C. April 8, 1926.

Herbert Hoover

"Peace can be promoted by the limitation of arms, but it will become a reality only through self-restraint and active effort in friendliness and helpfulness."
> —Inaugural Address. March 4, 1929.

Franklin Roosevelt

"Friendship calls for constructive efforts to muster the forces of humanity in order that an atmosphere of close understanding and cooperation may be cultivated. It involves mutual obligations and responsibilities, for it is only by sympathetic respect for the rights of others and a scrupulous fulfillment of the corresponding obligations by each member of the community that a true fraternity can be maintained."
> —Address on the Occasion of the Celebration of
> Pan-American Day, Washington. April 12, 1933.

"The spirit of the good neighbor is a practical and living fact. The twenty-one American Republics are not only living together in friendship and in peace; they are united in the determination so to remain."
    —Speech in Chautauqua, N.Y. August 14, 1936.

"We need the continuing friendship of our Allies in the war. And we shall need that friendship in the peace."
    —Radio Address. January 6, 1945.

Harry Truman

"To build a foundation of enduring peace we must work in harmony with our friends abroad and have the united support of our people. With Divine guidance, and your help, we will find the new passage to a far better world, a kindly and friendly world, with just and lasting peace."
    —Address to a Joint Session of the Congress. April 16, 1945.

Dwight Eisenhower

"Our policy, dedicated to making the free world secure, will envision all peaceful methods and devices--except breaking faith with our friends. We shall never acquiesce in the enslavement of any people in order to purchase fancied gain for ourselves."
    —Annual Message to the Congress on the State of the
        Union. February 2, 1953.

John Kennedy

"Geography has made us neighbors. History has made us friends."
    —Address before the Canadian Parliament in Ottawa.
        May 17, 1961.

"Support any friend and oppose any foe to assure the survival and the success of liberty."
    —Inaugural Address. January 20, 1961.

Lyndon Johnson

"Those who test our courage will find it strong, and those who seek our friendship will find it honorable. We will demonstrate anew that the strong can be just in the use of strength; and the just can be strong in the defense of justice."
　　—Address before a Joint Session of the Congress.
　　　November 27, 1963.

Richard Nixon

"Just to keep the record clear, in my book all of our friends are 'big shots.'"
　　—Statement at a Reception for Campaign Workers.
　　　January 21, 1969.

Gerald Ford

"We stand by our commitments and we will live up to our responsibilities in our formal alliances, in our friendships, and in our improving relations with potential adversaries."
　　—Address to a Joint Session of the Congress. August 12, 1974.

Jimmy Carter

"When combined, the small individual contributors of caring, friendship, forgiveness, and love, each of us different from our next-door neighbors, can form a phalanx, an army, with great capability."
　　—From his Book, *Our Endangered Values* (2005).[5]

Ronald Reagan

"Many times I wanted to stop and reach out from behind the glass, and connect. My friends: We did it. We weren't just marking time. We made a difference."
　　—Farewell Address. January 11, 1989.

George H.W. Bush

"Our friendship grew out of a shared belief you have to try to help whenever and wherever you can. I do think our friendship has sent a message around the world that just because you disagree on something doesn't mean you can't work together."
—Interview with Richard Dunham. March 18, 2011.[6]

Bill Clinton

"And the urgent question of our time is whether we can make change our friend and not our enemy."
—Inaugural Address. January 20, 1993.

George W. Bush

"When a friend stumbles and falls, you pick him up."
—In His Essay on *Friendship* (2004).

"It is through friendship that I have always succeeded, and which will give me the keys to survival today."
—In his Essay on *Friendship* (2004).

"We will stand up for our friends in the world."
—Statement to the American Jewish Committee.
   May 3, 2001.

Barack Obama

"It is the kindness to take in a stranger when the levees break, the selflessness of workers who would rather cut their hours than see a friend lose their job, which sees us through our darkest hours."
—Inaugural Address January 20, 2009.

"I am confident that the friendship between our nations will

continue to grow in the years ahead."
—Statement on Kosovo Independence Day. February 17, 2011.

"Know that America is a friend of each nation and every man, woman, and child who seeks a future of peace and dignity, and that we are ready to lead once more."
—Inaugural Address. January 20, 2009.

"We will be relentless in defense of our citizens and our friends and allies."
—White House Transcript. May 1, 2011.

---

1   Paraphrased.
2   Paraphrased.
3   Paraphrased.
4   Vol. 86. *Forbes* (1960).
5   Pg. 186. *Our Endangered Values* (2005).
6   Response to a question on why he was friends with Bill Clinton.

CHAPTER THIRTEEN

God

George Washington

"Let us raise a standard to which the wise and honest can repair; the rest is in the hands of God."
—Quoted by Gerald Ford during a speech to the Summit Conference on Inflation. September 28, 1974.

"It is impossible to rightly govern a nation without God and the Bible."
—Statement made during his Farewell Address. September 17, 1796.[1]

John Adams

"Power always thinks that it is doing God's service when really it is violating all his laws."
—Letter to Thomas Jefferson. February 2, 1816.

Thomas Jefferson

"Question with boldness even the existence of a God; because, if

there be one, he must more approve of the homage of reason, than that of blindfolded fear."
—Letter to Peter Carr. August 10, 1787.

"I tremble for my country when I reflect that God is just; that his justice cannot sleep forever."
—In His *Notes on Virginia* (1782).

"The God, who gave us life, gave us liberty at the same time."
—In his tract, *Rights of British America* (1774).

"It does me no injury for my neighbor to say there are twenty gods or no God."
—*Notes on Virginia* (1782).

Martin Van Buren

"There is a power in public opinion in this country—and I thank God for it."
—Speech at the U.S. Senate. December 5, 1837.

John Tyler

"Let it be henceforth proclaimed to the world that man's conscience was created free; that he is no longer accountable to his fellow man for his religious opinions, he being responsible therefore only to his God."
—Funeral Oration on the Death of Thomas Jefferson.
    July 11, 1826.

James Polk

"Under the benignant providence of Almighty God the representatives of the States and of the people are again brought together to deliberate for the public good."
—Fourth Annual Message. December 5, 1848.

Millard Fillmore

"May God save the country, for it is evident that the people will not."
 —Letter to Henry Clay. November 11, 1844.

Franklin Pierce

"I humbly invoke the God of our fathers for wisdom and firmness."
 —Inaugural Address. March 4, 1857.

Abraham Lincoln

"As God gives us to see the right, let us strive on to finish the work we are in."
 —Inaugural Address. March 4, 1865.

"Sir, my concern is not whether God is on our side; my greatest concern is to be on God's side, for God is always right."
 —*Bioletti Pamphlett* (1830).[2]

"In great contests each party claims to act in accordance with the will of God. Both may be, and one must be wrong."
 —Meditation on the Divine Will. September 30, 1862.

"Surely God would not have created such a being as man, with an ability to grasp the infinite, to exist only for a day! No, no, man was made for immortality."
 —Statement in Chicago. Fall 1857.

"God must love the common man, he made so many of them."
 —Conversation with Secretary John Hay.
   December 23, 1863.

Rutherford Hayes

"Conscience is the authentic voice of God to you."
　—Letter to son Scott R. Hayes. March 8, 1892.

Benjamin Harrison

"We Americans have no commission from God to police the world."
　—Statement to Congress. 1888.[3]

William Taft

"I love judges, and I love courts. They are my ideals that typify on earth what we shall meet hereafter in heaven under a just God."
　—Address in Pocatello, Idaho. October 5, 1911.

Woodrow Wilson

"No one can worship God on an empty stomach."
　—Speech in New York. May 23, 1912.

Warren Harding

"It is my conviction that the fundamental trouble with the people of the United States is that they have gotten too far away from Almighty God."
　—*New York Times*. April 2, 1922.

John Kennedy

"Those whom God has so joined together, let no man put asunder."
　—Address before the Canadian Parliament in Ottawa.
　　May 17, 1961.[4]

Lyndon Johnson

"This private unity of public men and their God is an enduring

source of reassurance for the people of America."
—*Liberty: a Magazine of Religious Freedom* (1965).[5]

Jimmy Carter

"I've never detected any conflict between God's will and my political duty. If you violate one, you violate the other."
—Quoted by Philip Jenkins in *Decade of Nightmares: The End of the Sixties and the Making of Eighties America* (2006).[6]

Ronald Reagan

"Freedom prospers when religion is vibrant and the rule of law under God is acknowledged."
—Statement at the Annual Convention of the National Association of Evangelicals in Orlando, Florida. March 8, 1983.

"Without God, democracy will not and cannot long endure."
—Remark at an Ecumenical Prayer Breakfast, Dallas, Texas. August 23, 1984.

"We are never defeated unless we give up on God."
—Quoted by Son Michael Reagan in 2011.[7]

"If we ever forget that we are One Nation Under God, then we will be a nation gone under."
—Statement at an Ecumenical Prayer Breakfast in Dallas, Texas. August 23, 1984.

Bill Clinton

"Part of our essential humanity is paying respect to what God gave us."
—Address on the 150th Anniversary of the Department of the Interior. March 4, 1999.

George W. Bush

"Freedom and fear, justice and cruelty, have always been at war, and we know that God is not neutral between them."
  —Address before a Joint Session of the Congress on the United States. September 20, 2001.

" I believe that God has planted in every heart the desire to live in freedom."
  —Address before a Joint Session of the Congress on the State of the Union. January 20, 2004.

Barack Obama

"We worship an awesome God in the Blue States."
  —Speech at the Democratic National Convention. July 24, 2004.

---

1   Scholars disagree to the veracity of this exact choice of words. Nevertheless, it is very well-known that Washington uttered similar pietistic remarks on numerous occasions.
2   Vol. 6. *Bioletti Pamphlett* (1830).
3   Caroline T. Hamsberger, *Treasury of Presidential Quotations* (1964).
4   Official United States embassy in Canada states "nature" in place of "God," whereas the *Oxford Dictionary of American Quotations* (2006) maintains the quote as listed above.
5   Vols. 60-62. *Liberty: a Magazine of Religious Freedom* (1965).
6   Pg. 175. *Decade of Nightmares: The End of the Sixties and the Making of Eighties America* (2006).
7   http://www.reagan.com.

CHAPTER FOURTEEN

Government

George Washington

"It may be laid down as a primary position, and the basis of our system, that every Citizen who enjoys the protection of a Free Government, owes not only a proportion of his property, but even of his personal services to the defense of it."
—Letter to Alexander Hamilton. May 2, 1783.

"Government is not reason; it is not eloquent; it is force. Like fire, it is a dangerous servant and a fearful master."
—Quoted in the *Christian Science Journal* (1902).[1]

"It is impossible to rightly govern a nation without God and the Bible."
—Statement made during his Farewell Address. September 17, 1796.[2]

"The marvel of all history is the patience with which men and women submit to burdens unnecessarily laid upon them by their governments."[3]

"The administration of justice is the firmest pillar of government."
　—Letter to U.S. Attorney General Edmund Randolph.
　　September 27, 1789.

"Mankind, when left to themselves, are unfit for their own government."
　—Letter to Henry Lee. October 31, 1786.

"The basis of our political system is the right of the people to make and to alter their constitutions of government."
　—Farewell Address. September 19, 1796.

John Adams

"The essence of a free government consists in an effectual control of rivalries."
　—*Discourses on Davila*, No. 13 (1790).

"There is danger from all men. The only maxim of a free government ought to be to trust no man living with power to endanger the public liberty."
　—From His *Notes for an Oration at Braintree*. Spring 1772.

"Our Constitution was made only for a moral and religious people. It is wholly inadequate to the government of any other."
　—Letter to the Officers of the First Brigade of the Third
　　Division of the Militia of Massachusetts. October 11, 1798.

"The happiness of society is the end of government."
　—Meeting with George Wythe. January 1776.

"The best form of government communicates ease, comfort, security, or, in one word, happiness, to the greatest number of persons."
　—Meeting with George Wythe. January 1776.

"While all other sciences have advanced, that of government is at a standstill—little better understood, little better practiced now than three or four thousand years ago."
—Letter to Thomas Jefferson. July 9, 1813.

"A government of laws, and not of men."
—*Boston Review*. January 1807.

"Fear is the foundation of most governments."
—Meeting with George Wythe. January 1776.

Thomas Jefferson

"I own that I am not a friend to a very energetic government. It is always oppressive."
—Letter to James Madison. December 20, 1787.

"I predict future happiness for Americans if they can prevent the government from wasting the labors of the people under the pretense of taking care of them."
—Reported by Stephen D. Hanson in *Transcending Time with Thomas Jefferson* (2010).[4]

"The spirit of resistance to government is so valuable on certain occasions that I wish it to be always kept alive."
—Letter to Abigail Adams. February 22, 1787.

"I have no fear that the result of our experiment will be that men may be trusted to govern themselves without a master."
—Letter to David Hartley. July 2, 1787.

"That government is the strongest of which every man feels himself a part."
—Letter to Governor Tiffin. February 2, 1807.

"The care of human life and happiness, and not their destruction, is the first and only object of good government."
—Speech in Washington County, Maryland. March 31, 1809.

"No government ought to be without censors; and where the press is free no one ever will."
—Letter to George Washington. September 9, 1792.

"A wise and frugal government, which shall leave men free to regulate their own pursuits of industry and improvement, and shall not take from the mouth of labor the bread it has earned—this is the sum of good government."
—Inaugural Address. March 4, 1801.

"Whenever the people are well-informed, they can be trusted with their own government."
—Richard Price. January 8, 1789.

"Sometimes it is said that man cannot be trusted with the government of himself. Can he, then be trusted with the government of others? Or have we found angels in the form of kings to govern him? Let history answer this question."
—Inaugural Address. March 4, 1801.

"Were it left to me to decide whether we should have a government without newspapers, or newspapers without a government, I should not hesitate a moment to prefer the latter."
—Letter to Col. Edward Carrington. January 16, 1787.

"Every government degenerates when trusted to the rulers of the people alone. The people themselves are its only safe depositories."
—In his *Notes on Virginia* (1782).

"Experience hath shown that even under the best forms of government those entrusted with power have, in time, and by slow operations, perverted it into tyranny."
—In his *Diffusion Of Knowledge Bill* (1779).

"I have no ambition to govern men; it is a painful and thankless office."
—Letter to John Adams. December 28, 1796.

"History, in general, only informs us of what bad government is."
—Letter to John Norvell. June 11, 1807.

"It is error alone which needs the support of government. Truth can stand by itself."
—In *Notes on the State of Virginia* (1782).

James Madison

"If men were angels, no government would be necessary."
—*The Federalist* February 6, 1788.[5]

"The rights of persons, and the rights of property, are the objects, for the protection of which Government was instituted."
—Speech at the Virginia Constitutional Convention. December 2, 1829.

"Knowledge will forever govern ignorance; and a people who mean to be their own governors must arm themselves with the power which knowledge gives."
—Letter to W. T. Barry. August 4, 1822.

"To suppose that any form of government will secure liberty or happiness without any virtue in the people is a chimerical idea."
—Speech in the Virginia Ratifying Convention on the Judicial Power. June 20, 1788.

"The people are the only legitimate fountain of power, and it is from them that the constitutional charter is derived."
—*The Federalist*. February 2, 1788.

"I have no doubt but that the misery of the lower classes will be found to abate whenever the Government assumes a freer aspect."
—Letter to Thomas Jefferson. June 19, 1786.

"The essence of Government is power; and power, lodged as it must be in human hands, will ever be liable to abuse."
—Speech at the Virginia Constitutional Convention. December 2, 1829.

"What is government itself but the greatest of all reflections on human nature."
—*The Federalist*, January 6, 1788.

"A popular government without popular information or the means of acquiring it, is but a prologue to a farce, or a tragedy, or perhaps both."
—Letter to W. T. Barry. August 4, 1822.

"In framing a government which is to be administered by men over men you must first enable the government to control the governed; and in the next place oblige it to control itself."
—*The Federalist*, January 6, 1788.

James Monroe

"Never did a government commence under auspices so favorable, nor ever was success so complete."
—Inaugural Address, in Reference to Recently-Formed U.S. Government. March 4, 1817.

"The best form of government is that which is most likely to prevent the greatest sum of evil."
  —Quoted by Anthony St. Peter in *The Greatest Quotations of All-Time* (2010).[6]

Andrew Jackson

"There are no necessary evils in government. Its evils exist only in its abuses."
  —In his Veto Message. July 10, 1832.

"Our government is founded upon the intelligence of the people."
  —Statement to Nicholas Trist. Fall 1836.

"The people are the government, administering it by their agents; they are the government, the sovereign power."
  —Proclamation 43. December 10, 1832.

"As long as our government is administered for the good of the people, and is regulated by their will; as long as it secures to us the rights of persons and of property, liberty of conscience and of the press, it will be worth defending."
  —Inaugural Address. March 4, 1829.

"We are beginning a new era in our government. I cannot too strongly urge the necessity of a rigid economy and an inflexible determination not to enlarge the income beyond the real necessities of the government."
  —Fifth Annual Message. December 3, 1833.

"The duty of government is to leave commerce to its own capital and credit as well as all other branches of business, protecting all in their legal pursuits, granting exclusive privileges to none."
  —Letter to William Lewis. December 28, 1841.

"Money is power, and in that government which pays all the public officers of the states will all political power be substantially concentrated."
—Veto Message. December 4, 1833.

Martin Van Buren

"The less government interferes with private pursuits, the better for general prosperity."
—Speech to the Senate and House of Representatives. September 4, 1837.

"In a government whose distinguishing characteristic should be a diffusion and equalization of its benefits and burdens the advantage of individuals will be augmented at the expense of the community at large."
—Second Annual Message. December 3, 1838.

"The government should not be guided by temporary excitement, but by sober second thought."
—*Weekly Globe*. September 14, 1843.

William Harrison

"The only legitimate right to govern is an express grant of power from the governed."
—Inaugural Address. March 4, 1841.

"I contend that the strongest of all governments is that which is most free."
—Letter to Bolivar. September 7, 1829.

"All the measures of the Government are directed to the purpose of making the rich richer and the poor poorer."
—Campaign Speech. October 1, 1840.

"Sir, I wish to understand the true principles of the Government. I wish them carried out. I ask nothing more."
—Last Words Before His Death. April 4, 1841.[7]

John Tyler

"So far as it depends on the course of this government, our relations of good will and friendship will be sedulously cultivated with all nations."
—Special Session Message. June 1, 1841.

Millard Fillmore

"'Friendly relations with all, but entangling alliances with none,' has long been a maxim with us. Our true mission is not to propagate our opinions or impose upon other countries our form of government by artifice or force, but to teach by example and show by our success, moderation, and justice the blessings of self-government and the advantages of free institutions."
—Second Annual Message. December 2, 1851.

James Polk

"The passion for office among members of Congress is very great, if not absolutely disreputable, and greatly embarrasses the operations of the Government. They create offices by their own votes and then seek to fill them themselves."
—Diary. June 22, 1846.

Franklin Pierce

"A Republic without parties is a complete anomaly. The histories of all popular governments show absurd is the idea of their attempting to exist without parties."
—Quoted by Joslyn Pine in *American Wit and Wisdom* (2002).[8]

"Administer government with vigilant integrity and rigid economy; cultivate peace and friendship with foreign nations, and demand and exact equal justice from all."
—Second Annual Message. December 4, 1854.

"The dangers of a concentration of all power in the general government of a confederacy so vast as ours are too obvious to be disregarded."
—Inaugural Address. March 4, 1853.

"Eschew intermeddling with the national policy and the domestic repose of other governments, and repel it from our own."
—Second Annual Message. December 4, 1854.

Abraham Lincoln

"Any people anywhere, being inclined and having the power, have the right to rise up, and shake off the existing government, and form a new one that suits them better. This is a most valuable—a most sacred right—a right, which we hope and believe, is to liberate the world."
—Speech to House of Representatives. January 12, 1848.

"This country, with its institutions, belongs to the people who inhabit it. Whenever they shall grow weary of the existing government, they can exercise their constitutional right of amending it, or exercise their revolutionary right to overthrow it."
—First Inaugural Address. March 4, 1861.

"The people will save their government, if the government itself will allow them."
—Special Session Message. July 4, 1861.

"No man is good enough to govern another man without that other's consent."
—Speech in Peoria, Illinois. October 16, 1854.

"Government of the people, by the people, for the people, shall not perish from the Earth."
—Gettysburg Address. November 19, 1863.

"The philosophy of the school room in one generation will be the philosophy of government in the next."
—Quoted by John Chalfant in *America—A Call to Greatness* (1999).[9]

Andrew Johnson

"Who, then, will govern? The answer must be, Man—for we have no angels in the shape of men, as yet, who are willing to take charge of our political affairs."
—First Inaugural Address. October 17, 1853.

"The goal to strive for is a poor government but a rich people."
—Quoted in 1845, as sourced from Elizabeth Jewell in *U.S. Presidents Fact Book* (2005).[10]

James Garfield

"The chief duty of government is to keep the peace and stand out of the sunshine of the people."
—Letter to H. N. Eldridge. December 14, 1869.

"All free governments are managed by the combined wisdom and folly of the people."
—Letter to B. A. Hinsdale. April 21, 1880.

Grover Cleveland

"In the scheme of our national government, the presidency is preeminently the people's office."
—In His *Independence of the Executive* (1913).[11]

"The lesson should be constantly enforced that though the people support the Government, Government should not support the people."
—*Public Opinion*. February 26, 1887.

"A government for the people must depend for its success on the intelligence, the morality, the justice, and the interest of the people themselves."
—*The Christian Register*. June 23, 1898.

Benjamin Harrison

"No other people have a government more worthy of their respect and love or a land so magnificent in extent, so pleasant to look upon, and so full of generous suggestion to enterprise and labor."
—Inaugural Address. March 4, 1889.

Theodore Roosevelt

"Behind the ostensible government sits enthroned an invisible government owing no allegiance and acknowledging no responsibility to the people."
—Speech at the National Convention of the Progressive Party in Chicago. August 6, 1912.

William Taft

"A government is for the benefit of all the people."
—Veto of the Arizona Enabling Act. August 22, 1911.

"We are all imperfect. We cannot expect perfect government."
—Speech to the Board of Trade and Chamber of Commerce, Washington, D.C. May 8, 1909.

Woodrow Wilson

"The government, which was designed for the people, has got into the hands of the bosses and their employers, the special interests. An invisible empire has been set up above the forms of democracy."
—In His *The New Freedom* (1913).[12]

"Liberty has never come from Government. Liberty has always come from the subjects of it. The history of liberty is a history of limitations of governmental power, not the increase of it."
—Speech at New York Press Club. September 9, 1912.

"A little group of willful men, representing no opinion but their own, have rendered the great government of the United States helpless and contemptible."
—Statement to Senate. March 4, 1917.

"If there are men in this country big enough to own the government of the United States, they are going to own it."
—In His *The New Freedom*, Section 12 (1913).

"What we seek is the reign of law, based upon the consent of the governed and sustained by the organized opinion of mankind."
—Fourth of July Address at George Washington's Tomb, Mount Vernon, Virginia. July 4, 1918.

Warren Harding

"In the great fulfillment we must have a citizenship less concerned about what the government can do for it and more anxious about what it can do for the nation."
—Address at the Republican Convention in Chicago, Illinois. June 7, 1916.

"Our most dangerous tendency is to expect too much of government, and at the same time do for it too little."
—Inaugural Address. March 4, 1921.

"The success of our popular government rests wholly upon the correct interpretation of the deliberate, intelligent, dependable popular will of America."
—Inaugural Address. March 4, 1921.

Calvin Coolidge

"The government of the United States is a device for maintaining in perpetuity the rights of the people, with the ultimate extinction of all privileged classes."
—Speech on the Anniversary of the First Continental Congress, Philadelphia, Pennsylvania. September 25, 1924.

"The Government does not make the people, but the people make the Government."
—Autobiography. 1924.[13]

Herbert Hoover

"If the law is upheld only by government officials, then all law is at an end."
—State of the Union Address. December 3, 1929.

"When there is a lack of honor in government, the morals of the whole people are poisoned."
—*New York Times*. August 9, 1964.

"It is just as important that business keep out of government as that government keep out of business."
—Address on the 150th Anniversary of the Battle of Kings Mountain. October 7, 1930.[14]

Franklin Roosevelt

"The government is us; we are the government, you and I."
—Nomination Address. July 2, 1932.[15]

"No government can help the destinies of people who insist in putting sectional and class consciousness ahead of general weal."
—Annual Message to Congress. January 3, 1938.

"I believe that in every country the people themselves are more peaceably and liberally inclined than their governments."
—Letter to Arthur Murray. April 14, 1933.

"The United States Constitution has proved itself the most marvelously elastic compilation of rules of government ever written."
—*New York Times*. March 3, 1930.

"The only sure bulwark of continuing liberty is a government strong enough to protect the interests of the people, and a people strong enough and well enough informed to maintain its sovereign control over the government."
—Fireside Chat. April 14, 1938.

"No government can conscript cooperation."
—Annual Message to Congress. January 3, 1938.

"Let us never forget that government is ourselves and not an alien power over us. The ultimate rulers of our democracy are not a President and senators and congressmen and government officials, but the voters of this country."
—Address at Marietta, Ohio. July 8, 1938.

Harry Truman

"When you have an efficient government, you have a dictatorship."
—Address at Columbia University. April 28, 1959.

"Never forget that a society of self-governing men is more powerful, more enduring, more creative than any other kind of society, however disciplined, however centralized."
—Radio Report to the American People on the Potsdam Conference. August 9, 1945.

Dwight Eisenhower

"I like to believe that people in the long run are going to do more to promote peace than our governments."
—Radio and Television Broadcast with Prime Minister Macmillan in London. August 31, 1959.

"Indeed, I think that people want peace so much, that one of these days' governments had better get out of the way and let them have it."
—Statement to British Prime Minister Harold Macmillan. August 31, 1959.

John Kennedy

"My brother Bob doesn't want to be in government—he promised Dad he'd go straight."
—*U.S. News & World Report* (1962).[16]

Lyndon Johnson

"I am concerned about the whole man. I am concerned about what the people, using their government as an instrument and a tool, can do toward building the whole man, which will mean a better society and a better world."
—Statement on Medical Research. April 13, 1963.

Richard Nixon

"Sure there are dishonest men in local government. But there are dishonest men in national government too."

—Quoted by Maurice Charney in *Comedy High and Low* (1978).[17]

Gerald Ford

"Our great Republic is a government of laws and not of men."
  —Statement on Taking the Oath of Office. August 9, 1974.

"No government, no matter how well-intentioned, can take the place of the family in the scheme of things."
  —Speech at the Conclusion of the International Eucharistic Congress in Philadelphia, Pennsylvania. August 8, 1976.

"Truth is the glue that holds government together."
  —Statement on Taking the Oath of Office. August 9, 1974.

"A government big enough to give you everything you want is a government big enough to take from you everything you have."
  —Address to Joint Session of the Congress. August 12, 1974.

Jimmy Carter

"Government is a contrivance of human wisdom to provide for human wants. People have the right to expect that these wants will be provided for by this wisdom."
  —In his *A Government as Good as Its People* (1996).[18]

Ronald Reagan

"Government is not the solution to our problem; government is the problem."
  —First Inaugural Address. January 20, 1981.

"Today, if you invent a better mousetrap, the government comes along with a better mouse."
  —Statement during White House Briefing for Members of the Magazine Publishers Association. March 14, 1985.

"Government always finds a need for whatever money it gets."
—Speech at a Fundraising Dinner for Governor James R. Thompson, Jr., in Chicago. July 7, 1981.

"The most terrifying words in the English language are: I'm from the government and I'm here to help."
—The President's News Conference. August 12, 1986.

"Government does not solve problems; it subsidizes them."
—Speech. December 11, 1972.

"Protecting the rights of even the least individual among us is basically the only excuse the government has for even existing."

"Man is not free unless government is limited."
—Farewell Address to the Nation. January 11, 1989.

"Government exists to protect us from each other."
—Quoted by R. Scott Fosler in *The New Economic Role of American States* (1990).[19]

"No government ever voluntarily reduces itself in size."
—Televised Address. October 27, 1964.

"Government is like a baby. An alimentary canal with a big appetite at one end and no sense of responsibility at the other."
—*The New York Times*. November 14, 1965.

"Governments tend not to solve problems, only to rearrange them."
—In His *The Reagan Wit* (1998).[20]

"One way to make sure crime doesn't pay would be to let the government run it."
—Speech to the California State Bar in Dallas, Texas. October 26, 1967.

"The taxpayer—that's someone who works for the federal government but doesn't have to take the civil service examination."
—*Life*. January 21, 1966.[21]

"The best minds are not in government. If any were, business would steal them away."
—Joking Statement on *Information Week* (1998).[22]

"Government is the people's business and every man, woman and child becomes a shareholder with the first penny of tax paid."
—Remarks at the New York City Partnership Luncheon in New York January 14, 1982.

"The problem is not that people are taxed too little; the problem is that government spends too much."
—Address before a Joint Session of Congress on the State of the Union. January 27, 1987.

"Government's first duty is to protect the people, not run their lives."
—Address Before a Joint Session of the Tennessee State Legislature in Nashville, Tennessee. March 15, 1982

"People do not make wars; governments do."
—Session with Students and Faculty at Moscow State University. May 31, 1988.

Bill Clinton

"The new rage is to say that the government is the cause of all our problems, and if only we had no government, we'd have no problems. I can tell you that contradicts evidence, history, and common sense."
—Speech to students at Hillsborough Community College, Tampa, Florida. March 30, 1995.

George W. Bush

"We believe ranchers and farmers and family business owners can make better decisions about the future than the government can."
—Remarks on the Office of Management and Budget Mid-Session Review. July 11, 2007.

"You can spend your money better than the government can spend your money."
—Speech in Erie, Pennsylvania. June 17, 2009.

"Government does not create wealth. The major role for the government is to create an environment where people take risks to expand the job rate in the United States."
—Speech in Erie, Pennsylvania. June 17, 2009.

Barack Obama

"If the people cannot trust their government to do the job for which it exists—to protect them and to promote their common welfare—all else is lost."
—Speech at the University of Nairobi. August 28, 2006.

"It's time to fundamentally change the way that we do business in Washington. To help build a new foundation for the 21st century, we need to reform our government so that it is more efficient, more transparent, and more creative. That will demand new thinking and a new sense of responsibility for every dollar that is spent."
—The President's Weekly Address. April 25, 2009.

---

1   Vol. 20, pg. 465. *Christian Science Journal* (1902).
2   Scholars disagree to the veracity of this exact quote. Nevertheless, it is very well-known that Washington uttered pietistic remarks on numerous occasions.
3   This particular quote was uttered by Senator William Borah of Idaho, and

whether he borrowed it from Washington is debatable. Nevertheless, it correctly sums up Washington's endeavors to start a revolution against government tyranny. One may also view his letter to the "The Roman Catholics in the United States," composed on May 15, 1790.

4   Pg.125. *Transcending Time with Thomas Jefferson* (2010).

5   No. 51

6   Pg. 275. *The Greatest Quotations of All-Time* (2010).

7   Quoted by Jebediah Whitman in *A Memorial to Our Dear Departed President* (1841).

8   Pg. 40. *American Wit and Wisdom* (2002).

9   Pg. 166. *America—A Call to Greatness* (1999).

10   Pg. 134. *U.S. Presidents Fact book* (2005).

11   Pg. 9. *Independence of the Executive* (1913).

12   Pg. 35. *The New Freedom* (1913).

13   *Calvin Coolidge, His Ideals of Citizenship As Revealed Through his Speeches and Writings* (W. A. Wilde Company), pg. 30.

14   Hoover has been noted saying this quote at several occasions, verbatim or paraphrased.

15   Summarized.

16   Vol. 52. *U.S. News & World Report* (1962).

17   Pg. 27. *Comedy High and Low* (1978).

18   Pg. 5. *A Government as Good as Its People* (1996).

19   Pg. 233. *The New Economic Role of American States* (1990).

20   Pg. 42. *The Reagan Wit* (1998).

21   Pg. 74. *Life*. Jan. 21, 1966.

22   Issues 684-689.

CHAPTER FIFTEEN

Happiness

George Washington

"Happiness and moral duty are inseparably connected."
—Letter to the Episcopal Church. August 19, 1789.

John Adams

"The happiness of society is the end of government."
—Meeting with George Wythe. January 1776.

Thomas Jefferson

"I predict future happiness for Americans if they can prevent the government from wasting the labors of the people under the pretense of taking care of them."
—Reported by Stephen D. Hanson in *Transcending Time with Thomas Jefferson* (2010).[1]

"I find that he is happiest of whom the world says least, good or bad."
—Letter to John Adams. August 27, 1786.

"I do not take a single newspaper, nor read one a month, and I feel myself infinitely the happier for it."
—Letter to Tench Coxe. May 1, 1794.

"The care of human life and happiness, and not their destruction, is the first and only object of good government."
—Speech in Washington County, Maryland. March 31, 1809.

"Our greatest happiness does not depend on the condition of life in which chance has placed us, but is always the result of a good conscience, good health, occupation, and freedom in all just pursuits."
—*Notes on Virginia* (1782).

"Happiness is not being pained in body or troubled in mind."
—Letter to William Short. October 31, 1819.

"We hold these truths to be self-evident: that all men are created equal; that they are endowed by their Creator with certain unalienable rights; that among these are life, liberty, and the pursuit of happiness."
—Declaration of Independence. July 4, 1776.

"It is neither wealth nor splendor; but tranquility and occupation which give you happiness."
—Quoted by Lemuel Gulliver XVI in *Book Six: Our Psychological Motivations* (2008).

James Madison

"To suppose that any form of government will secure liberty or happiness without any virtue in the people is a chimerical idea."
—Speech in the Virginia Ratifying Convention on the Judicial Power. June 20, 1788.

"The class of citizens who provide at once their own food and their own raiment may be viewed as the most truly independent and happy."
　　—*National Gazette*. March 3, 1792.

James Monroe

"If we look to the history of other nations, ancient or modern, we find no example of a growth so rapid, so gigantic, of a people so prosperous and happy."
　　—First Inaugural Address. March 5, 1817.

Martin Van Buren

"As to the presidency, the two happiest days of my life were those of my entrance upon the office and my surrender of it."
　　—Quoted by Barbara Holland in *Hail to Chiefs* (1990).[2]

James Polk

"May the boldest fear and the wisest tremble when incurring responsibilities on which may depend our country's peace and prosperity, and in some degree the hopes and happiness of the whole human family."
　　—Inaugural Address. March 4, 1845.

James Buchanan

"Sir, if you are as happy entering the presidency as I am in leaving it, then you are truly a happy man."
　　—Statement to Abraham Lincoln on his Presidential
　　　Inauguration. March 4, 1861.

Abraham Lincoln

"Most folks are as happy as they make up their minds to be."

—Quoted by Dale Carnegie in *How to Win Friends and Influence People* (1936).[3]

Rutherford Hayes

"The independence of all political and other bother is a happiness."
—Diary. March 28, 1875.

Woodrow Wilson

"I am not sure that it is of the first importance that you should be happy. Many an unhappy man has been of deep service to himself and to the world."
—Address at Princeton University. June 7, 1908.

Franklin Roosevelt

"Happiness lies in the joy of achievement and the thrill of creative effort."
—First Inaugural Address. March 4, 1933.

Lyndon Johnson

"I have learned that only two things are necessary to keep one's wife happy. First, let her think she's having her own way. And second, let her have it."
—Toast to Princess Margaret. November 17, 1965.

Jimmy Carter

"For this generation, ours, life is nuclear survival, liberty is human rights, the pursuit of happiness is a planet whose resources are devoted to the physical and spiritual nourishment of its inhabitants."
—Farewell Address to the Nation. January 14, 1981.

1   Pg. 125. *Transcending Time with Thomas Jefferson* (2010) by Stephen D. Hanson.
2   Pg. 65. *Hail to Chiefs* (1990) by Barbara Holland.
3   Pg. 68 (according to revised 1998 edition). *How to Win Friends and Influence People* by Dale Carnegie.

CHAPTER SIXTEEN

History

George Washington

"The marvel of all history is the patience with which men and women submit to burdens unnecessarily laid upon them by their governments." [1]

Thomas Jefferson

"I like the dreams of the future better than the history of the past."
    —Letter to John Adams. August 1, 1816.

"History, in general, only informs us of what bad government is."
    —Letter to John Norvell. June 11, 1807.

James Madison

"Do not separate text from historical background. If you do, you will have perverted and subverted the Constitution, which can only end in a distorted, bastardized form of illegitimate government."
    —*The Federalist*. January 19, 1788.[2]

James Monroe

"If we look to the history of other nations, ancient or modern, we find no example of a growth so rapid, so gigantic, of a people so prosperous and happy."
—First Inaugural Address. March 5, 1817.

Franklin Pierce

"We have nothing in our history or position to invite aggression; we have everything to beckon us to the cultivation of relations of peace and amity with all nations."
—Inaugural Address. March 4, 1853.

James Garfield

"Few men in our history have ever obtained the presidency by planning to obtain it."
—Diary. February 4, 1879.

Benjamin Harrison

"There never has been a time in our history when work was so abundant or when wages were as high."
—Fourth Annual Message. December 6, 1892.

William McKinley, Jr.

"That's all a man can hope for during his lifetime—to set an example—and when he is dead, to be an inspiration for history."
—Statement to George Cortelyou, Cortelyou's Diary. December 29, 1899.

Theodore Roosevelt

"Never throughout history has a man who lived a life of ease left a name worth remembering."

—Statement to the New York State Agricultural
   Association, Syracuse, NY. September 7, 1903.[3]

Woodrow Wilson

"The history of liberty is a history of limitations of governmental power, not the increase of it."
   —Speech at New York Press Club. September 9, 1912.

"There is little for the great part of the history of the world except the bitter tears of pity and the hot tears of wrath."
   —Speech in Oakland, California. September 18, 1919.

"The history of liberty is a history of resistance."
   —Speech at New York Press Club. September 9, 1912.

Franklin Roosevelt

"The point in history at which we stand is full of promise and danger."
   —Message to Congress. February 12, 1945.

Harry Truman

"Men make history and not the other way around."
   —Quoted by Gregory K. Morris in *In Pursuit of Leadership* (2003).

"Study men, not historians."
   —Letter to Edward Harris. July 19, 1950.

"To hell with them. When history is written they will be the sons of bitches—not I."
   —Diary. December 6, 1952.

"There is nothing new in the world except the history you do not know."
—In His *Mr. President* (1952).[4]

"Nixon is one of the few in the history of this country to run for high office talking out of both sides of his mouth at the same time and lying out of both sides."
—*The Bulletin* (1973).[5]

Dwight Eisenhower

"The history of free men is never really written by chance but by choice; their choice!"
—Address in Pittsburgh. October 9, 1956.

"We are in a fast-running current of the great stream of history. Heroic efforts will long be needed."
—Address at the Opening of the NATO Meetings in Paris. December 16, 1957.

"Things have never been more like the way they are today in history."
—Quoted by Michael Hoskin in *History of Science* (1985).[6]

"Neither a wise man nor a brave man lies down on the tracks of history to wait for the train of the future to run over him."
—*Time*. October 6, 1952.

"History does not long entrust the care of freedom to the weak or the timid."
—Inaugural Address. January 20, 1953.

John Kennedy

"History is a relentless master. It has no present, only the past rushing into the future. To try to hold fast is to be swept aside."

—Summation of Speech at Dinner Honoring Representative Albert Thomas in Houston. November 21, 1963.

"In the long history of the world, only a few generations have been granted the role of defending freedom in its hour of maximum danger. I do not shrink from this responsibility—I welcome it."
   —Inaugural Address. January 20, 1961.

"We have the power to make this the best generation of mankind in the history of the world--or to make it the last."
   —Address before the 18th General Assembly of the United Nations. September 20, 1963.

"We would like to live as we once lived. But history will not permit it."
   —Statement at the Breakfast of the Fort Worth Chamber of Commerce. November 22, 1963.

Lyndon Johnson

"No one single decision can make life suddenly better or can turn history around for the good."
   —Speech at Montgomery County Fair, Dayton, Ohio. September 5, 1966.

Richard Nixon

"The greatest honor history can bestow is the title of peacemaker."
   —Inaugural Address. January 20, 1969.

"Once you get into this great stream of history, you can't get out."
   —Quoted by Earl Mazo in *Richard Nixon: A Political and Personal Portrait* (1959).[7]

"My own view is that taping of conversations for historical purposes was a bad decision."
—*Director* (1974).[8]

"Each moment in history is a fleeting time, precious and unique."
—Inaugural Address. January 20, 1969.

"I don't think that a leader can control his destiny if the forces of history are running in another direction."
—In *The Kiwanis Magazine* (1968).[9]

Gerald Ford

"History and experience tell us that moral progress comes not in comfortable and complacent times, but out of trial and confusion."
—Address before Joint Session of Congress.
January 19, 1976.

Jimmy Carter

"The awareness that health is dependent upon habits that we control makes us the first generation in history that to a large extent determines its own destiny."
—In His *Everything to Gain* (1987).[10]

"Take part in the stream of history. Study the course of history."
—Speech at Cheyney State College, Pennsylvania.
May 20, 1979.

Ronald Reagan

"History teaches that war begins when governments believe the price of aggression is cheap."
—Address from the White House on United States-Soviet Relations. January 16, 1984.

George H. W. Bush

"I see history as a book with many pages, and each day we fill a page with acts of hopefulness and meaning. The new breeze blows, a page turns, the story unfolds. And so today a chapter begins, a small and stately story of unity, diversity, and generosity—shared, and written, together."
—Inaugural Address. January 20, 1989.

George W. Bush

"Americans are rising to the tasks of history, and they expect the same of us."
—Address before Joint Session of Congress.
January 20, 2004.

"I'm going to put people in my place, so when the history of this administration is written at least there's an authoritarian voice saying exactly what happened."
—*Associated Press*. March 17, 2009.

"Now, there are some who would like to rewrite history—revisionist historians is what I like to call them."
—*CNN*. June 16, 2003.

---

1   One may also view Washington's letter to the "The Roman Catholics in the United States," composed on May 15, 1790. The above-mentioned quote was uttered by Senator William Borah of Idaho, and whether he borrowed it from Washington is debatable. Nevertheless, it correctly sums up Washington's endeavors to start a revolution against government tyranny.
2   No. 41. Summation of this article; exact quote maybe paraphrased.
3   Paraphrased comments during his speech to the agricultural association.
4   Pg. 81. *Mr. President* (1952).
5   Vol. 95. Part 4. *The Bulletin* (1973).
6   Vol. 23. Pg 299. *History of Science* (1985).
7   Pg. 157. *Richard Nixon: A Political and Personal Portrait* (1959).
8   Vol. 27. *Richard Nixon: A Political and Personal Portrait* (1959).
9   Vol. 53. *The Kiwanis Magazine* (1968).
10 Pg. 40. *Everything to Gain* (1987).

CHAPTER SEVENTEEN

Honor

George Washington

"I have no other view than to promote the public good, and am unambitious of honors not founded in the approbation of my Country."
    —Letter to Henry Laurens. January 31, 1778.

Thomas Jefferson

"The second office in the government is honorable and easy; the first is but a splendid misery."
    —Letter to Elbridge Gerry. May 13, 1797.

James Monroe

"National honor is the national property of the highest value."
    —First Inaugural Address. March 4, 1817.

Andrew Jackson

"Every good citizen makes his country's honor his own."
— Speech. Recorded by C. Bronson. 1845.

Millard Fillmore

"An honorable defeat is better than a dishonorable victory."
— Speech in Buffalo, New York. September 13, 1844.

Chester Arthur

"Honors to me now are not what they once were."
— Quoted by Thomas Reeves in *Gentleman Boss: the Life of Chester Alan Arthur* (1975).[1]

Grover Cleveland

"I have considered the pension list of the republic a roll of honor."
— Special Message to Congress. July 5, 1888.

"Honor lies in honest toil."
— Letter Accepting Nomination of the U.S. Presidency. August, 18, 1884.

Theodore Roosevelt

"The one thing I want to leave my children is an honorable name."
— Comment to Henry Cabot Lodge; quoted by Edward Renehan, Jr. in *The Lion's Pride* (1999).[2]

Calvin Coolidge

"No person was ever honored for what he received. Honor has been the reward for what he gave."
— In his *Have Faith in Massachusetts* (1919).[3]

Herbert Hoover

"No greater nor more affectionate honor can be conferred on an American than to have a public school named after him."
    —Remarks at Dedication of Herbert Hoover Junior High School, San Francisco, California. June 5, 1956.

"Honor is not the exclusive property of any political party."
    —*Frontier* (1951).[4]

"When there is a lack of honor in government, the morals of the whole people are poisoned."
    —*New York Times*. August 9, 1964.

Franklin Roosevelt

"Confidence thrives on honor."
    —First Inaugural Address. March 4, 1933.

Richard Nixon

"Your steadfastness in supporting our insistence on peace with honor has made peace with honor possible."
    —Address to the Nation Announcing Conclusion of an Agreement on Ending the War and Restoring Peace in Vietnam. January 23, 1973.

George H. W. Bush

"Leadership to me means duty, honor, country."
    —Quoted by Bryan Curtis in *A Call to America* (2002).

1   Pg. 159. *Gentleman Boss: the Life of Chester Alan Arthur* (1975).
2   Pg. 4. *The Lion's Pride* (1999).
3   Pg. 173. *Have Faith in Massachusetts* (1919).
4   Vol. 3. *Frontier* (1951).

CHAPTER EIGHTEEN

Hope

George Washington

"I hope I shall possess firmness and virtue enough to maintain what I consider the most enviable of all titles, the character of an honest man."
    —Letter to Alexander Hamilton. August 28, 1788.

John Adams

"When people talk of the freedom of writing, speaking or thinking I cannot choose but laugh. No such thing exists; but I hope it will."
    —Letter to Thomas Jefferson. July 15, 1817.

Thomas Jefferson

"My theory has always been that if we are to dream, the flatteries of hope are as cheap, and pleasanter, than the gloom of despair."
    —Letter to M. De Marbois. June 14, 1817.

"I hope our wisdom will grow with our power, and teach us, that the less we use our power the greater it will be."
　—Letter to Thomas Leiper. June 12, 1815.

James Madison

"Much is to be hoped from the progress of reason."
　—"Universal Peace" Essay. January 31, 1792.

John Q. Adams

"Posterity: you will never know how much it has cost my generation to preserve your freedom. I hope you will make good use of it."
　—As Referenced in the U.S. Congress, *Congressional Record.*
　　March 9, 1999.

Abraham Lincoln

"My dream is of a place and a time where America will once again be seen as the last best hope of earth."
　—Second Annual Message. December 1, 1862.[1]

"This is a most valuable—a most sacred right—a right, which we hope and believe, is to liberate the world."
　—Speech to House of Representatives. January 12, 1848.

"I hope to stand firm enough to not go backward, and yet not go forward fast enough to wreck the country's cause."
　—Letter to Zachariah Chandler. November 20, 1863.

"All that I am, or hope to be, I owe to my angel mother."
　—Quoted by Josiah Holland in *Life of Abraham Lincoln* (1866).

Rutherford Hayes

"Take counsel of hopes rather than of fears to win."
　—Diary. December 16, 1861.

William McKinley, Jr.

"That's all a man can hope for during his lifetime—to set an example—and when he is dead, to be an inspiration for history."
   —Statement to George Cortelyou, Cortelyou's Diary.
      December 29, 1899.

Woodrow Wilson

"You are not here merely to make a living. You are here in order to enable the world to live with a finer spirit of hope."
   —Address at Swarthmore College. October 25, 1913.

Calvin Coolidge

"Our great hope lies in developing what is good."
   —Address to *Associated Press*. April 22, 1924.

Herbert Hoover

"The pause between the errors and trials of the day and the hopes of the night."
   —Quoted by Daniel Okrent in *Last call: The Rise and Fall of Prohibition* (2010).[2]

Franklin Roosevelt

"We have always held to the hope, the belief, the conviction that there is a better life, a better world, beyond the horizon."
   —Address. Oct. 12, 1940.

Dwight Eisenhower

"Whatever America hopes to bring to pass in the world must first come to pass in the heart of America."
   —Inaugural Address. January 20, 1953.

John Kennedy

"We stand today on the edge of a new frontier—a frontier of unfulfilled hopes and threats."
—Address of Senator John F. Kennedy Accepting the Democratic Party Nomination for the Presidency of the United States. July 15, 1960.

Gerald Ford

"I would hope that understanding and reconciliation are not limited to the 19th hole alone."
—Quoted by Don Natta in *First off the Tee* (2003).[3]

Jimmy Carter

"We become not a melting pot but a beautiful mosaic. Different people, different beliefs, different yearnings, different hopes, different dreams."
—Department of Health, Education, and Welfare Remarks and a Question-and-Answer Session with Department Employees. February 16, 1977.

Ronald Reagan

"To sit back hoping that someday, some way, someone will make things right is to go on feeding the crocodile, hoping he will eat you last—but eat you he will."
—Quoted by Alton Pryor in *Little Known Tales in Nevada History* (2004).[4]

George W. Bush

"By bringing hope to the oppressed and delivering justice to the violent, they are making America more secure."
—State of the Union Address. January 20, 2004.

"Families are where our nation finds hope, where wings take dream."
　—Speech in LaCrosse, Wisconsin. October 18, 2000.

"I know there is a lot of ambition in Washington. But I hope the ambitious realize that they are more likely to succeed with success as opposed to failure."
　—Interview with *Associated Press*. January 18, 2001.

Barack Obama

"Do we participate in a politics of cynicism or a politics of hope?"
　—Address at the Democratic National Convention.
　　July 27, 2004.

1　Paraphrased: *Congressional Record*, V. 153, Pt. 12, June 18, 2007 to June 26, 2007. edited by Congress (U.S.).
2　Pg. 304. *Last Call: The Rise and Fall of Prohibition* (2010).
3　Pg. 153. *First off the Tee* (2003).
4　Pg. 19. *Little Known Tales in Nevada History* (2004) by Alton Pryor.

CHAPTER NINETEEN

Law

John Adams

"A government of laws, and not of men."
—*Boston Review*. January 1807.

Thomas Jefferson

"Laws made by common consent must not be trampled on by individuals."
—Letter to Garret Van Meter. April 27, 1781.

"Taste cannot be controlled by law."
—In his *Notes on a Money Unit* (1784).

"Law is often but the tyrant's will."
—Letter to Mr. Tiffany. April 4, 1819.

"It is more dangerous that even a guilty person should be punished without the forms of law than that he should escape."
—Letter to William Carmichael. May 27, 1788.

James Madison

"It will be of little avail to the people that the laws are made by men of their own choice if the laws be so voluminous that they cannot be read, or so incoherent that they cannot be understood."
    —*The Federalist*. February 27, 1788.[1]

Andrew Jackson

"The Constitution and the laws are supreme and the Union indissoluble."
    —Message to Congress. January 16, 1833.

Martin Van Buren

"If laws acting upon private interests cannot be avoided, they should be confined within the narrowest limits."
    —Second Annual Message. December 3, 1838.

Abraham Lincoln

"The best way to get a bad law repealed is to enforce it strictly."
    —Address before the Young Men's Lyceum of Springfield, Illinois. January 27, 1837.

Andrew Johnson

"Our Government springs from and was made for the people. Here there is no room for favored classes or monopolies; the principle of our Government is that of equal laws."
    —State of the Union Address. December 4, 1865.

"Most, if not all, of our domestic troubles are directly traceable to violations of the organic law."
    —Fourth State of the Union Address. December 9, 1868.

"The Constitution and the laws of the United States shall be the supreme law of the land."
　　—State of the Union Address. December 4, 1865.

Ulysses Grant

"I know no method to secure the repeal of bad or obnoxious laws so effective as their stringent execution."
　　—Inaugural Address. March 4, 1869.

Rutherford Hayes

"Law without education is a dead letter."
　　—Diary. January 23, 1883.

"With education the needed law follows without effort."
　　—Diary. January 23, 1883.

James Garfield

"A law is not a law without coercion behind it."
　　—Statement to Congress, as Recorded in His *From the Farm to the Presidential Chair* (1880).[2]

Grover Cleveland

"Public officers are the servants and agents of the people, to execute the laws which the people have made."
　　—Letter accepting the Nomination for Governor of New York. October 7, 1882.

"No man has ever yet been hanged for breaking the spirit of a law."
　　—Quoted by James Ford Rhodes in *History of the United States* (1919).

Theodore Roosevelt

"Obedience of the law is demanded; not asked as a favor."
—State of the Union Address. December 7, 1903.

"No man is above the law and no man is below it: nor do we ask any man's permission when we ask him to obey it."
—State of the Union Address. December 7, 1903.

"It is difficult to make our material condition better by the best law, but it is easy enough to ruin it by bad laws."
—Speech in Providence, Rhode Island. August 23, 1902.

William Taft

"We live in a stage of politics, where legislators seem to regard the passage of laws as much more important than the results of their enforcement."
—In his book, *Our Chief Magistrate and His Powers* (1916).[3]

"Action for which I become responsible, or for which my administration becomes responsible, shall be within the law."
—Letter to Gifford Pinchot. September 17, 1909.

Woodrow Wilson

"What we seek is the reign of law, based upon the consent of the governed and sustained by the organized opinion of mankind."
—Address on Mount Vernon, Virginia. July 4, 1918.

Calvin Coolidge

"Men speak of natural rights, but I challenge any one to show where in nature any rights existed or were recognized until there was established for their declaration and protection a duly promulgated body of corresponding laws."
—Speech in Northampton, Massachuetts. July 27, 1920.

"I sometimes wish that people would put a little more emphasis upon the observance of the law."
—Autobiography. 1924.[4]

"One with the law is a majority."
—*New York Times*. July 28, 1920.

Herbert Hoover

"If the law is upheld only by government officials, then all law is at an end."
—State of the Union Address. December 3, 1929.

Franklin Roosevelt

"We must lay hold of the fact that economic laws are not made by nature. They are made by human beings."
—Acceptance Speech in Chicago. July 2, 1932.

Dwight Eisenhower

"The clearest way to show what the rule of law means to us in every-day life is to recall what has happened when there is no rule of law."
—*The Nation*. May 5, 1958.

John Kennedy

"We prefer world law in the age of self-determination to world war in the age of mass extermination."
—Speech to the General Assembly of the United Nations. New York City. September 25, 1961.

Lyndon Johnson

"We have talked long enough in this country about equal rights. It is time now to write it in the books of law."
—Address before a Joint Session of the Congress. November 27, 1963.

Gerald Ford

"Our great Republic is a government of laws and not of men. Here, the people rule."
    —Statement on Taking the Oath of Office. August 9, 1974.

Ronald Reagan

"Freedom prospers when the rule of law under God is acknowledged."
    —Statement at the Annual Convention of the National
    Association of Evangelicals in Orlando, Florida.
    March 8, 1983.

"We must reject the idea that every time a law's broken, society is guilty rather than the lawbreaker. It is time to restore the American precept that each individual is accountable for his actions."
    —Republican National Convention. Miami, Florida.
    July 31, 1968.

George W. Bush

"States should have the right to enact laws."
    —Statement in Cleveland. June 29, 2000.

1   No. 62.
2   Pg. 129. *From the Farm to the Presidential Chair* (1880).
3   Pg. 12., *Our Chief Magistrate and His Powers* (1916).
4   *Calvin Coolidge, His Ideals of Citizenship As Revealed Through his Speeches and Writings* (W. A. Wilde Company), pg. 30.

CHAPTER TWENTY

Leadership

John Q. Adams

"If your actions inspire others to dream more, learn more, do more and become more, you are a leader."
—Quoted by Thomas Wurtz in *Corporate Common Sense* (2009).[1]

James Buchanan

"The test of leadership is not to put greatness into humanity, but to elicit it, for the greatness is already there."
—Referenced by the Association of the United States Army in *Army* (1963).[2]

Theodore Roosevelt

"Appraisals are where you get together with your team leader and agree what an outstanding member of the team you are, how much your contribution has been valued, what massive potential you have and, in recognition of all this, would you mind having your salary halved."
—From His *Outdoors and Indoors*, Published in 1920.[3]

"People ask the difference between a leader and a boss. The leader leads, and the boss drives."
—Speech in Binghamton, New York. October 24, 1910.

Woodrow Wilson

"The ear of the leader must ring with the voices of the people."
—Speech at the University of Tennessee. June 17, 1890.

"Absolute identity with one's cause is the first and great condition of successful leadership."
—*The Virginia Spectator* (1879).[4]

Harry Truman

"Progress occurs when courageous, skillful leaders seize the opportunity to change things for the better."
—Quoted by Gregory Morris in *In Pursuit of Leadership* (2006).[5]

"Leadership requires vision, courage and tolerance."
—Address to Congress. April 16, 1945.

"Where there is no leadership, society stands still."
—Quoted by Gregory Morris in *In Pursuit of Leadership* (2006).[6]

Dwight Eisenhower

"The people of the world genuinely want peace. Some day the leaders of the world are going to have to give in and give it to them."
—Statement to British Prime Minister Harold Macmillan. August 31, 1959.[7]

"The supreme quality for a leader is unquestionably integrity. Without it, no real success is possible, no matter whether it is on a section gang, a football field, in an army, or in an office."
—Quoted by John Maxwell in *Ultimate Leadership* (2007).[8]

"Though force can protect in emergency, only justice, fairness, consideration and cooperation can finally lead men to the dawn of eternal peace."
— *Life*. March 24, 1947.[9]

"You don't lead by hitting people over the head—that's assault, not leadership."
— In *New York State Education* (1967).[10]

"Leadership is the art of getting someone else to do something you want done because he wants to do it."
— Review for United States Bureau Employment Security (1956).[11]

"In order to be a leader a man must have followers. And to have followers, a man must have their confidence."
— Quoted by John Maxwell in *Ultimate Leadership* (2007).[12]

John Kennedy

"Leadership and learning are indispensable to each other."
— Speech Prepared for Delivery at the Trade Mart in Dallas, Texas. November 22, 1963.

"A nation which has forgotten the quality of courage is not as likely to insist upon that quality in its leaders."
— Quoted John Hellmann in *The Kennedy Obsession* (1999).[13]

Richard Nixon

"If an individual wants to be a leader and isn't controversial, that means he never stood for anything."
— Quoted by Bryan Curtis in *A Call to America* (2002).

"I don't think that a leader can control, to any great extent, his destiny."
—In *The Kiwanis Magazine* (1968). [14]

Jimmy Carter

"We cannot be both the world's leading champion of peace and the world's leading supplier of the weapons of war."
—Statement to Arms Control Association during 1976 Presidential Campaign.

George H. W. Bush

"Leadership to me means duty, honor, country. It means character, and it means listening from time to time."
—Quoted by Bryan Curtis in *A Call to America* (2002).

George W. Bush

"I have a different vision of leadership. A leadership is someone who brings people together."
—Statement on August 18, 2000.

"We can't allow the world's worst leaders to blackmail, threaten, and deprive freedom-loving nations of peace."
—*CNN*. September 5, 2002. [15]

Barack Obama

"We can't drive our SUVs and eat as much as we want and keep our homes on 72 degrees at all times and then just expect that other countries are going to say OK. That's not leadership. That's not going to happen."
—Waterfront Park Speech in Portland, Oregon. May 18, 2008.

"Americans still believe in an America where anything's possible
—they just don't think their leaders do."
    —Speech at the 'Take Back America' conference,
        Washington D.C. June 13, 2006.

1   Pg. 256. *Corporate Common Sense* (2009).
2   Vol. 14. *Army* (1963).
3   This quote is commonly attributed to Theodore Roosevelt. While the quote is not verbatim in *Outdoors and Indoors*, it does summarize the message of sacrifice contained therein.
4   Pg. 366. *The Virginia Spectator* (1879).
5   Pg. 21. *In Pursuit of Leadership* (2006).
6   Pg. 21.
7   An alternate quote of Truman reads, "Indeed, I think that people want peace so much, that one of these days governments had better get out of the way and let them have it."
8   Pg. 286. *Ultimate Leadership* (2007).
9   Pg. 89. *Life*. March 24, 1947.
10 Vol. 55. *New York State Education* (1967).
11 Employment *Security Review*: Vol. 23.
12 Pg. 286. *Ultimate Leadership* (2007).
13 Pg. 79. *The Kennedy Obsession* (1999).
14 Vol. 53. *The Kiwanis Magazine* (1968).
15 Summarized.

CHAPTER TWENTY-ONE

Liberty

George Washington

"Arbitrary power is most easily established on the ruins of liberty abused to licentiousness."
—Circular to the States. June 8, 1783.

"Liberty, when it begins to take root, is a plant of rapid growth."
—Letter to James Madison. March 2, 1788.

"It will be found an unjust and unwise jealousy to deprive a man of his natural liberty upon the supposition he may abuse it."
—Quoted by Oliver Cromwell about Washington.[1]

"The preservation of the sacred fire of liberty and the destiny of the republican model of government are entrusted to the hands of the American people."
—Inaugural Address. April 30, 1789.

John Adams

"The only maxim of a free government ought to be to trust no man living with power to endanger the public liberty."
　　—From His *Notes for an Oration at Braintree*. Spring 1772.

"I must study politics and war that my sons may have liberty to study mathematics and philosophy."
　　—Letter to Abigail Adams. May 12, 1780.

"Liberty implies thought and choice and power."
　　—In a Collection of Letters to John Taylor. Dated April 15, 1814 April 8, 1824.

"Liberty cannot be preserved without general knowledge among the people."
　　—In his *A Dissertation on the Canon and Feudal Law* (1765).

Thomas Jefferson

"The tree of liberty must be refreshed from time to time with the blood of patriots and tyrants."
　　—Letter to William Stephens Smith. November 13, 1787.

"The boisterous sea of liberty is never without a wave."
　　—Letter to Richard Rush. October 20, 1820.

"I would rather be exposed to the inconveniences attending too much liberty than those attending too small a degree of it."
　　—Letter to Edward Rutledge. August 25, 1791.

"The God, who gave us life, gave us liberty at the same time."
　　—In His Tract, *Rights of British America* (1774).

"The natural progress of things is for liberty to yield."
　　—Statement to Edward Carrington. May 27, 1788.

"Educate and inform the whole mass of the people. They are the only sure reliance for the preservation of our liberty."
—Letter to James Madison. December 20, 1787.

"Rightful liberty is unobstructed action according to our will within limits drawn around us by the equal rights of others."
—Letter to Isaac Tiffany. April 4, 1819.

"Timid men prefer the calm of despotism to the tempestuous sea of liberty."
—Letter to M. Mazzei. April 24, 1796.

"We are not to expect to be translated from despotism to liberty in a featherbed."
—Letter to Gilbert du Motier. April 2, 1790.

"In every country and every age, the priest had been hostile to Liberty."
—Letter to Horatio Spafford. March 17, 1814.

"We hold these truths to be self-evident: that all men are created equal; that they are endowed by their Creator with certain unalienable rights; that among these are life, liberty, and the pursuit of happiness."
—Declaration of Independence. July 4, 1776.

"It behooves every man who values liberty for himself, to resist invasions of it in the case of others."
—Letter to Dr. Benjamin Rush. April 21, 1808.

James Madison

"What spectacle can be more edifying or more seasonable, than that of Liberty and Learning, each leaning on the other for their mutual and surest support?"
—Letter to W. T. Barry. August 4, 1822.

"The advancement and diffusion of knowledge is the only guardian of true liberty."
—Letter to George Thomson. June 30, 1825.

"To suppose that any form of government will secure liberty or happiness without any virtue in the people is a chimerical idea."
—Speech in the Virginia Ratifying Convention on the Judicial Power. June 20, 1788.

"Liberty may be endangered by the abuse of liberty, but also by the abuse of power."
—*The Federalist*. March 1, 1788.[2]

"The happy Union of these States is a wonder; their Constitution a miracle; their example the hope of Liberty throughout the world."
—Letter to Samuel Kercheval. September 7, 1829.

"We are right to take alarm at the first experiment upon our liberties."
—In His *Memorial and Remonstrance*, a message to the General Assembly of the Commonwealth of Virginia. June 20, 1785.

James Monroe

"Our country may be likened to a new house. We lack many things, but we possess the most precious of all—liberty!"
—In *American Anecdotes* (1830).

John Q. Adams

"Nip the shoots of arbitrary power in the bud, is the only maxim which can ever preserve the liberties of any people."
—*Novanglus Essay*. Published in 1775.[3]

Andrew Jackson

"I weep for the liberty of my country when I see at this early day of its successful experiment that corruption has been imputed to many members of the House of Representatives, and the rights of the people have been bartered for promises of office."
—Letter to John Coffee. February 19, 1825.

"They are the bone and sinew of the country men who love liberty and desire nothing but equal rights and equal laws."
—Farewell Address. March 4, 1837.

"As long as our government secures to us the rights of persons and of property, liberty of conscience and of the press, it will be worth defending."
—Inaugural Address. March 4, 1829.

James Buchanan

"Liberty must be allowed to work out its natural results; and these will, ere long, astonish the world."
—Letter to Mr. Slidell. November 10, 1845.

Abraham Lincoln

"Our defense is in the preservation of the spirit which prizes liberty. Destroy this spirit and you have planted the seeds of despotism."
—Speech in Edwardsville, Illinois. September 11, 1858.

"Fourscore and seven years ago our fathers brought forth on this continent, a new nation, conceived in Liberty."
—The Gettysburg Address, Gettysburg, Pennsylvania. November 19, 1863.

Theodore Roosevelt

"Order without liberty and liberty without order are equally destructive."
—Speech in Baltimore, Maryland. September 28, 1918.

Woodrow Wilson

"Liberty has never come from Government. Liberty has always come from the subjects of it."
—Speech at New York Press Club. September 9, 1912.

"The history of liberty is a history of limitations of governmental power, not the increase of it."
—Speech at New York Press Club. September 9, 1912.

"America was established not to create wealth but to realize a vision, to realize an ideal—to discover and maintain liberty among men."
—Speech to Chicago Democrat's Iroquois Club, February 12, 1912.

"The world must be planted upon the tested foundations of political liberty."
—Address to Congress for a Declaration of War Against Germany. April 2, 1917.

"I would rather belong to a poor nation that was free than to a rich nation that had ceased to be in love with liberty."
—Address before the Southern Commercial Congress at Mobile, Alabama. October 27, 1913.

"The history of liberty is a history of resistance."
—Speech at New York Press Club. September 9, 1912.

Franklin Roosevelt

"The only sure bulwark of continuing liberty is a government strong enough to protect the interests of the people, and a people strong enough and well enough informed to maintain its sovereign control over the government."
 —Fireside Chat. April 14, 1938.

Dwight Eisenhower

"Love of liberty means the guarding of every resource that makes freedom possible--from the sanctity of our families and the wealth of our soil to the genius of our scientists."
 —First Inaugural address. January 20, 1953.

"Kinship among nations is not determined in such measurements as proximity of size and age, but by his liberty to speak and act as he sees fit, subject only to provisions that he trespass not upon similar rights of others."
 —London Guild Hall Address. June 12, 1945.

"Vigilance and sacrifice are the price of liberty."
 —Speech to the American Society of Newspaper Editors.
     April 16, 1953.

"The eyes of the world are upon you. The hopes and prayers of liberty-loving people everywhere march with you."
 —Message to Troops before Normandy Landings.
     June 2, 1944.

John Kennedy

"Let every nation know, whether it wishes us well or ill, that we shall pay any price, bear any burden, meet any hardship, support any friend, oppose any foe to assure the survival and the success of liberty."
 —Inaugural Address. January 20, 1961.

Jimmy Carter

"Liberty is human rights."
—Farewell Address to the Nation. January 14, 1981.

Ronald Reagan

"Concentrated power has always been the enemy of liberty."
—Radio Address in 1978.[4]

George W. Bush

"I believe in the transformational power of liberty."
—Presidential Debate with John Kerry in Coral Gables,
    Florida. September 30, 2004.

Barack Obama

"I know my country has not perfected itself. At times, we've struggled to keep the promise of liberty and equality for all of our people."
—Speech in Berlin, Germany. July 24, 2008.

1   No. 3.
2   No. 63.
3   Although commonly attributed to Washington (as in Glen Beck's *Seven Wonders That Will Change Your Life*, 2011) this quote was actually written by Oliver Cromwell in a letter to the governor of Edinburgh Castle on September 12, 1650. That being said, this quote does embody Washington's disposition to liberty being the birthright for every individual.
4   *Policy Review* (1982). Heritage Foundation, Washington, D.C.

CHAPTER TWENTY-TWO

Life

George Washington

"Labor to keep alive in your breast that little spark of celestial fire, called conscience."
 —Written in the 1740s in One of His School Books.

"I attribute all my success in life to the moral, intellectual and physical education I received from my mother."
 —Cited by George W. Bush in his Proclamation 7674— Mother's Day, 2003. May 7, 2003.

John Adams

"There are two educations. One should teach us how to make a living and the other how to live." [1]

Thomas Jefferson

"My only fear is that I may live too long. This would be a subject of dread to me."
 —Letter to Philip Mazzei. March 17, 1801.

"I cannot live without books."
—Letter to John Adams. 1815.

"The earth belongs to the living, not to the dead."
—Letter to John Eppes. June 24, 1813.

"It is in our lives and not our words that our religion must be read."
—Letter to Mrs. M. Harrison Smith. August 6, 1816.

"The care of human life and happiness, and not their destruction, is the first and only object of good government."
—Speech in Washington County, Maryland. March 31, 1809.

"The God, who gave us life, gave us liberty at the same time."
—In His Tract, *Rights of British America* (1774).

"Our greatest happiness does not depend on the condition of life in which chance has placed us, but is always the result of a good conscience."
—In His *Notes on Virginia*. 1782.

"Friendship is precious; not only in the shade, but in the sunshine of life, and thanks to a benevolent arrangement the greater part of life is sunshine."
—Letter to Maria Cosway. 1786.

"We hold these truths to be self-evident: that all men are created equal; that they are endowed by their Creator with certain unalienable rights; that among these are life, liberty, and the pursuit of happiness."
—Declaration of Independence. July 4, 1776.

Andrew Jackson

"I feel in the depths of my soul that it is the highest, most sacred, and most irreversible part of my obligation to preserve the union of these states, although it may cost me my life."
—Second Inaugural address, March 4, 1833.

Martin Van Buren

"We will not tolerate an incompetent or unworthy man to hold in his weak or wicked hands the lives and fortunes of his fellow-citizens."
>—Quoted by biographer William Holland in *The Life and Political Opinions of Martin Van Buren* (1835).

Abraham Lincoln

"I like to see a man live so that his place will be proud of him."
>—Paraphrased from the Gettysburg Address. November 19, 1863.[2]

"I am bound to live by the light that I have."
>—Quoted by U.S. Congress, *Congressional Record*. February 27, 1907.[3]

"In the end, it's not the years in your life that count. It's the life in your years."
>—Referenced by Barack Obama. Statement during the State Dinner Honoring Prime Minister Manmohan Singh of India. November 24, 2009.

Rutherford Hayes

"As friends go it is less important to live."
>—Diary. July 8, 1887.

James Garfield

"Man cannot live by bread alone; he must have peanut butter."[4]

"I have had many troubles in my life, but the worst of them never came."
>—Quoted in *The Lutheran Standard* (1969).[5]

Chester Arthur

"I may be President of the United States, but my private life is nobody's damned business."
 —Response to a Temperance Reformer Who Asked if He Drank.[6]

Benjamin Harrison

"Great lives never go out; they go on."
 —*British Columbia Medical Journal* (1964).[7]

William McKinley, Jr.

"That's all a man can hope for during his lifetime—to set an example—and when he is dead, to be an inspiration for history."
 —Statement to George Cortelyou, Cortelyou's Diary.
 December 29, 1899.

Theodore Roosevelt

"Never throughout history has a man who lived a life of ease left a name worth remembering."
 —Statement to the New York State Agricultural Association, Syracuse, NY. September 7, 1903.[8]

"Far better is it to dare mighty things and to win glorious triumphs, even though checkered by failure than to rank with those poor spirits who neither enjoy nor suffer much, because they live in a gray twilight."
 —Speech before the Hamilton Club, Chicago, Illinois.
 April 10, 1899.

"Some men can live up to their loftiest ideals without ever going higher than a basement."
 —Quoted by Austin O'Malley in *Keystones of Thought* (1914).[9]

"Far and away the best prize that life has to offer is the chance to work hard at work worth doing."
 —"Square Deal" Labor Day Speech in Syracuse, New York. September 7, 1903.

"No man is worth his salt who is not ready at all times to risk his well-being, to risk his body, to risk his life, in a great cause."
 —*American Printer and Lithographer* (1916).[10]

"I wish to preach, not the doctrine of ignoble ease, but the doctrine of the strenuous life."
 —Speech before the Hamilton Club, Chicago, Illinois. April 10, 1899.

Woodrow Wilson

"You are not here merely to make a living. You are here to enrich the world."
 —Address at Swarthmore College. October 25, 1913.

Calvin Coolidge

"To live under the American Constitution is the greatest political privilege that was ever accorded to the human race."
 —Address at the White House. December 12, 1924.

"There is no dignity quite so impressive, and no one independence quite so important, as living within your means."
 —From His Autobiography (1929).[11]

Franklin Roosevelt

"If civilization is to survive, we must cultivate the science of human relationships—the ability of all peoples, of all kinds, to live together, in the same world at peace."
 —Undelivered Jefferson Day Address. April 13, 1945.

"We have always held to the hope, the belief, the conviction that there is a better life, a better world, beyond the horizon."
—Address. Oct. 12, 1940.

Harry Truman

"In reading the lives of great men, I found that the first victory they won was over themselves: self-discipline came first."
—Diary. May 14, 1934.

"All my life, whenever it comes time to make a decision, I make it and forget about it."
—Comment Made to a Reporter in 1958.[12]

Dwight Eisenhower

"An old man complained about life and about all of the joys of youth and middle age that he was now missing…well, considering when you were born, if you weren't old, you'd be dead!"[13]
—The President's News Conference. September 7, 1960.

"The clearest way to show what the rule of law means to us in everyday life is to recall what has happened when there is no rule of law."
—*The Nation*. May 5, 1958.

John Kennedy

"We must never forget that the highest appreciation is not to utter words, but to live by them."
—*Presbyterian Outlook* (1963).[14]

"Do not pray for easy lives. Pray to be stronger men."
—Speech at the 11th Annual Presidential Prayer Breakfast. February 7, 1963.

"We would like to live as we once lived."
    —Statement at the breakfast of the Fort Worth Chamber of
    Commerce. November 22, 1963.

"A man may die, nations may rise and fall, but an idea lives on."
    —Remarks Recorded for the Opening of a USIA Transmitter
    at Greenville, North Carolina. February 8, 1963.

"Change is the law of life. And those who look only to the past
or present are certain to miss the future."
    —Address in the Assembly Hall at the Paulskirche in
    Frankfurt. June 25, 1963.

"Once you say you're going to settle for second, that's what happens to you in life."
    —In Regard to Post of Vice Presidency. Oft-Repeated
    Statement Made During His 1960 Presidential
    Campaigns.

"The courage of life is often a less dramatic spectacle than the
courage of a final moment; but it is no less a magnificent mix-
ture of triumph and tragedy."
    —Inaugural Ceremony. January 20, 1961.

"There is always inequality in life. Life is unfair."
    —Statement during Press Conference. March 21, 1962.

Lyndon Johnson

"We live in a world that has narrowed into a neighborhood
before it has broadened into a brotherhood."
    —Speech at the Lighting of the Nation's Christmas Tree.
    December 22, 1963.

"No one single decision can make life suddenly better or can turn history around for the good."
    —Speech at Montgomery County Fair, Dayton.
        September 5, 1966.

"I'd rather give my life than be afraid to give it."
    —*NATO Letter* (1964).[15]

"Life as we know it with its humanity is more unique than many have thought. And we must remember this."
    —Remarks upon Viewing New Mariner 4 Pictures from
        Mars. July 29, 1965.

Jimmy Carter

"We will not learn how to live together in peace by killing each other's children."
    —Acceptance Speech for the Nobel Peace Prize.
        December 10, 2002.

"We should live our lives as though Christ were coming this afternoon."
    —Statement to Bible Class, Marantha Baptist Church,
        Plains, Georgia. March 1976.

Ronald Reagan

"God's greatest gift is human life."
    —Radio Address to the Nation. January 22, 1983.

"My philosophy of life is that if we make up our mind what we are going to make of our lives, then work hard toward that goal, we never lose—somehow we win out."
    —Quoted by Louise Boone in *Contemporary Business* (1987).[16]

"Some people wonder all their lives if they've made a difference."
  —Letter to Lance Cpl. Joe Hickey. September 23, 1983.

"While I take inspiration from the past, like most Americans, I live for the future."
  —Address to the Republican National Convention in
    Houston. August 17, 1992.

"We have the duty to protect the life of an unborn child."
  —Radio Address to the Nation. January 22, 1983.

"There's purpose and worth to each and every life."
  —Statement in Opening Ceremony of Ronald Reagan
    Library. November 4, 1991.

"Life is one grand, sweet song, so start the music."
  —Words Reagan Wrote in His High School Senior Yearbook
    in 1928.

George W. Bush

"I believe that God has planted in every heart the desire to live in freedom."
  —Address before a Joint Session of the Congress on the
    State of the Union. January 20, 2004.

"States should have the right to enact laws to end the inhumane practice of ending a life that otherwise could live."
  —Statement in Cleveland. June 29, 2000.

Barack Obama

"We need to steer clear of this poverty of ambition, where people want to drive fancy cars and wear nice clothes and live in nice

apartments but don't want to work hard to accomplish these things."
—*Obama, In His Own Words* (2008).[17]

"Focusing your life solely on making a buck shows a certain poverty of ambition. It asks too little of yourself. Because it's only when you hitch your wagon to something larger than yourself that you realize your true potential."
—Commencement Address at Knox College, Galesburg, Illinois. June 4, 2005.

1　Though this statement may have very well symbolized Adams' philosophy of life, the literal quote is most often attributed to American historian and essayist James Truslow Adams in *To "Be" or to "Do"* in *Forum*, June 1929. Vol. LXXXI, no. 6.
2　Common-known alternative: "I like to see a man proud of the place in which he lives."
3　Pg. 4176. *Congressional Record*. February 27, 1907.
4　It is debatable whether this quote was uttered by Garfield. Nevertheless, it is a play on Matthew 4:14: "Man shall not live by bread alone, but by every word that proceedeth out of the mouth of God."
5　Vol. 9. *The Lutheran Standard* (1969).
6　Reeves, Thomas. *Gentleman Boss: The Life of Chester Alan Arthur* (1975), ch. 8.
7　Vol. 6. *British Columbia Medical Journal* (1964).
8　Paraphrased comments during his speech to the agricultural association.
9　Pg. 117 *Keystones of Thought*. 1914. Debate remains whether this was O'Malley's own concoction, or if he really heard these words from Roosevelt. Nevertheless, the quote does support the strenuous and exciting life Roosevelt lived during those formidable years.
10　Vol. 62. pg. 49. *Keystones of Thought* (1914).
11　*Autobiography of Calvin Coolidge*, pg. 159.
12　Please see *Recent America, A History* (1963) by Henry Parkes and *The Presidential Character* (1985) by James Barber for more background information and full quote.
13　Paraphrased.
14　Vol. 145. Issue 41. *Presbyterian Outlook* (1963).
15　Vol. 12. *NATO Letter* (1964).
16　Pg. 725. *Contemporary Business* (1987).
17　Pg. 11. Edited by Carl Palmieri. Obama, *In His Own Words* (2008).

CHAPTER TWENTY-THREE

Love

John Adams

"A desire to be beloved, by his fellows is one of the earliest as well as the keenest dispositions discovered in the heart of man."
—In His *Discourses on Davila* (1790).[1]

"As much as I converse with sages and heroes, they have very little of my love. I prefer the Delights of a Garden to the Dominion of a World."
—Letter to Abigail Adams. March 16, 1777.

"A government of our own choice, managed by persons whom we love, revere, and can confide in, has charms in it for which men will fight."
—Letter to Abigail Adams. May 17, 1776.

Andrew Jackson

"Love liberty."
—Farewell Address. March 4, 1837.

Abraham Lincoln

"God must love the common man, he made so many of them."
  —Conversation with Secretary John Hay.
    December 23, 1863.

Theodore Roosevelt

"The man who loves other countries as much as his own stands on a level with the man who loves other women as much as he loves his own wife."
  —Address Delivered in City Hall, New York.
    September 6, 1918.

William Taft

"I love judges, and I love courts."
  —Address in Pocatello, Idaho. October 5, 1911.

Woodrow Wilson

"No one can love his neighbor on an empty stomach."
  —Speech in New York. May 23, 1912.

Franklin Roosevelt

"There is nothing I love as much as a good fight."
  —*New York Times*. January 22, 1911.

Richard Nixon

"People react to fear, not love; they don't teach that in Sunday school, but it's true."
  —Quoted by William Safire in *Before the Fall* (1977). [2]

Gerald Ford

"There are no adequate substitutes for father, mother, and children bound together in a loving commitment to nurture and protect. No government, no matter how well-intentioned, can take the place of the family in the scheme of things."

   —Speech at the Conclusion of the International Eucharistic Congress in Philadelphia, Pennsylvania. August 8, 1976.

Ronald Reagan

"If we love our country, we should also love our countrymen."
   —Inaugural Address. January 20, 1981.

Barack Obama

"My parents shared not only an improbable love; they shared an abiding faith in the possibilities of this nation. They would give me an African name, Barack, or blessed, believing that in a tolerant America your name is no barrier to success."
   —Speech at the Democratic National Convention.
   July 27, 2004.

1   No. 4.
2   Pg. 8. *Before the Fall* (1977), by William Safire.

CHAPTER TWENTY-FOUR

Mind

John Adams

"Old minds are like old horses; you must exercise them if you wish to keep them in working order."
    —Statement to House Representative Josiah Quincy.[1]

"Prepare your mind for your fate."
    —Letter to Benjamin Rush. April 12, 1809.

Thomas Jefferson

"The general mind must be strengthened by education."
    —Letter to Van der Kemp. July 9, 1820.

"Bodily decay is gloomy in prospect, but of all human contemplations the most abhorrent is body without mind."
    —Letter to John Adams. August 1, 1816.

"Power is not alluring to pure minds."
    —Letter to Mr. Melish. January 13, 1813.

"The natural cause of the human mind is certainly from creduli-ty to skepticism."
—Letter to Dr. Casper Wistar. June 21, 1807.

"A strong body makes the mind strong."
—Letter to Peter Carr. August 19, 1785.

"Enlighten the people generally, and tyranny and oppressions of body and mind will vanish like evil spirits at the dawn of day."
—Letter to Dupont de Nemours. April 24, 1816.

"Happiness is not being pained in body or troubled in mind."
—Letter to William Short. October 31, 1819.

"He who knows nothing is closer to the truth than he whose mind is filled with falsehoods and errors."
—Letter to John Norvell. June 11, 1807.

"I believe that every human mind feels pleasure in doing good to another."
—Letter to John Adams. October 14, 1816.

James Madison

"The capacity of the female mind for studies of the highest order cannot be doubted, having been sufficiently illustrated by its works of genius, of erudition, and of science."
—Letter to Albert Picket. September 1821.

"Religious bondage shackles and debilitates the mind and unfits it for every noble enterprise, every expanded prospect."
—Letter to Mr. William Bradford, Jr. April 1, 1774.

Abraham Lincoln

"Always bear in mind that your own resolution to succeed is

more important than any other."
—Letter to Isham Reavis on November 5, 1855.

"Most folks are as happy as they make up their minds to be."
—Quoted by Dale Carnegie in *How to Win Friends and Influence People* (1936).[2]

"Some single mind must be master, or else there will be no agreement in anything."
—Letter to W. M. Fishback. February 17, 1864.

"All my life I have tried to pluck a thistle and plant a flower wherever the flower would grow in thought and mind."
—Statement to Joshua Speed.[3]

Andrew Johnson

"It's a damn poor mind that can only think of one way to spell a word."
—Presumed Retort to John Quincy Adams (1833).[4]

Grover Cleveland

"Let us constantly bear in mind that our country is something which, as an example and interpreter of freedom, belongs to the world, and which, in its blessed mission, belongs to humanity."
—Address at the Jewelers' Association Annual Dinner, New York. November 21, 1890.

"Bear in mind that you may labor and toil in the whirl and excitement of business to build new warehouses and add to the city's wealth and to your own, but that while you thus build, ignorant, negligent, or corrupt men among your lawmakers can easily and stealthily pull them down."
—Speech at Evacuation Day Celebration, New York. November 26, 1883.

"Political duty and selfish interests lead in the same direction."
—Speech at Evacuation Day Celebration, New York.
November 26, 1883.

Theodore Roosevelt

"The boy who is going to make a great man must not make up his mind merely to overcome a thousand obstacles, but to win in spite of a thousand repulses and defeats."
—In an Article Published in *The Outlook*. March 31, 1900.

"Great thoughts speak only to the thoughtful mind, but great actions speak to all mankind."[5]

"I ask it not for my sake, not the least in the world, but for the sake of common country, that they make up their minds to speak only the truth."
—Speech at Milwaukee, Wisconsin. October 14, 1912.

"To educate a man in mind and not in morals is to educate a menace to society."
—Quoted by Gerald Ford in His Commencement Address at Warner Pacific College in Portland. May 23, 1976.

Franklin Roosevelt

"Men are not prisoners of fate, but only prisoners of their own minds."
—Pan American Day Address. April 15, 1939.

Harry Truman

"When even one American—who has done nothing wrong—is forced by fear to shut his mind and close his mouth—then all Americans are in peril."
—Address at the Dedication of the New Washington Headquarters of the American Legion. August 14, 1951.

"Those who want the Government to regulate matters of the mind and spirit are like men who are so afraid of being murdered that they commit suicide to avoid assassination."
   —Address at the National Archives Dedicating the New Shrine for the Declaration of Independence, the Constitution, and the Bill of Rights. December 15, 1952.

John Kennedy

"The human mind is our fundamental resource."
   —Special Message to the Congress on Education. February 20, 1961.

Ronald Reagan

"My philosophy of life is that if we make up our mind what we are going to make of our lives, then work hard toward that goal, we never lose—somehow we win out."
   —Quoted by Louise Boone in *Contemporary Business* (1987).[6]

"There are no constraints on the human mind, except those we ourselves erect."
   —State of the Union Address. February 6, 1985.

"The best minds are not in government. If any were, business would steal them away."
   —Joking Statement on *Information Week* (1998).

1   Child, Lydia Maria: *Looking Toward Sunset: From Sources Old and New, Original and Selected*, pg. 431.
2   Pg. 68 (according to revised 1998 edition) *How to Win Friends and Influence People* by Dale Carnegie.
3   In a letter of Mr. Speed's dating from December 6, 1866. See Abraham Lincoln by William Herndon and Jesse Weik, pg. 231.
4   Commonly-reported retort to his political rival, John Quincy Adams, after the latter boycotted Harvard University's bestowing of a Doctorate of Laws degree on Jackson on June 27, 1833, stating "I would not be present to witness her

[Harvard's] disgrace in conferring her highest literary honors on a barbarian who could not write a sentence of grammar and could hardly spell his own name." Alternate version of Jackson's quote: "It's a damn poor mind, indeed, which can't think of at least two ways to spell a word."

5   Though this quote may have been the exact words of Roosevelt (as several scholars concur), the quote verbatim is known to have been uttered by American social worker Emily Bissell. Nevertheless, the quote does embody Roosevelt's many social undertakings, and several of his sayings are actual variants of this particular quote.

6   Pg. 725. *Contemporary Business* by Louise Boone.

CHAPTER TWENTY-FIVE

Money

John Adams

"All the perplexities, confusion and distress in America arise, not from defects in their Constitution or Confederation, not from want of honor or virtue, so much as from the downright ignorance of the nature of coin, credit and circulation."
—Letter to Thomas Jefferson. August 23, 1787.

Thomas Jefferson

"Money, not morality, is the principle commerce of civilized nations."
—Letter (1810).

"Never spend your money before you have earned it."
—From His *A Decalogue of Canons for Observation in Practical Life*. February 21, 1825.

"The glow of one warm thought is to me worth more than money."
—Letter to C. McPherson. February 25, 1773.

"To compel a man to furnish contributions of money for the propagation of opinions which he disbelieves is sinful and tyrannical."
—Report to General Assembly. June 18, 1779.

"I hope we shall crush in its birth the aristocracy of our moneyed corporations which dare already to challenge our government to a trial by strength, and bid defiance to the laws of our country."
—Letter to George Logan. November 12, 1816.

"People will forget themselves except in the sole faculty of making money."
—In *Notes on the State of Virginia* (1782).

"Give up money give up fame give up science give the earth itself and all it contains rather than do an immoral act."
—Letter to Peter Carr. August 19, 1785.

James Madison

"The circulation of confidence is better than the circulation of money."
—On the Subject of "Power of Judiciary." June 20, 1788.

"It is vain to wait for money."
—On the Subject of "Power of Judiciary." June 20, 1788.

Andrew Jackson

"Mischief springs from the power which the moneyed interest derives."
—Farewell Address. March 4, 1837.

"Money is power."
—Veto Message. December 4, 1833.

"Public money is but a species of public property."
—Message to the Senate Protesting Censure Resolution. April 15, 1834.

"The duty of government is to leave commerce to its own capital and credit."
—Letter to William Lewis. December 28, 1841.

Martin Van Buren

"The application of public money by an officer of Government to private uses should be made a felony and visited with severe and ignominious punishment."
—Second Annual Message. December 4, 1838.

"A system which can in a time of profound peace, when there is a large revenue laid by, thus suddenly prevent the application and the use of the money of the people in the manner and for the objects they have directed cannot be wise."
—Special Session Message. September 4, 1837

Franklin Pierce

"Remember that time is money."
—One of the Morals of Chapter Six in His Book, *The Tariff and the Trusts* (1909).

"No more money should be collected than is necessary for the wants of government."
—*The Tariff and the Trusts* (1909).[1]

Abraham Lincoln

"I can make more generals, but horses cost money."
—Quoted by James Wilson in *Under the Old Flag* (1912).[2]

"My money is my own!"
   —Speech Delivered at Cooper Institute, New York.
      February 27, 1860.[3]

James Garfield

"Whoever controls the volume of money in any country is absolute master of all industry and commerce."
   —March 1899. Reported in *Money*.[4]

"He who controls the money supply of a nation controls the nation."
   —*The Nation*. December 18, 1873.[5]

"Government is an artificial giant, and the power that moves it is money."
   —Speech to the House of Representatives. March 5, 1874.

"As I work, I want my money to work."
   —Address to the House of Representatives.
      November 16, 1877.

Chester Arthur

"The extravagant expenditure of public money is an evil not to be measured by the value of that money to the people who are taxed for it."
   —Statement to the House of Representatives. August 1, 1882.

Herbert Hoover

"Let me remind you that credit is the lifeblood of business, the lifeblood of prices and jobs."
   —Address at the Coliseum in Des Moines, Iowa.
      October 4, 1932.

Ronald Reagan

"Government always finds a need for whatever money it gets."
—Speech at a Fundraising Dinner for Governor James R. Thompson, Jr., in Chicago. July 7, 1981.

George W. Bush

"You can spend your money better than the government can spend your money."
—Speech in Erie, Pennsylvania. June 17, 2009.

Barack Obama

"We need earmark reform, and when I'm President, I will go line by line to make sure that we are not spending money unwisely."
—Presidential Debate at the University of Mississippi. September 26, 2008.

"I don't take a dime of their [lobbyist] money, and when I am president, they won't find a job in my White House."
—Campaign Speech in Spartanburg, South Carolina. November 3, 2007.

"Money is not the only answer, but it makes a difference."
—*Obama, In His Own Words* (2008).[6]

"It's time to fundamentally change the way that we do business in Washington. That will demand new thinking and a new sense of responsibility for every dollar that is spent."
—The President's Weekly Address. April 25, 2009.

1   Pg. 267. *The Tariff and the Trusts* (1909).
2   Pg. 349. *Under the Old Flag* (1912) by James Wilson.
3   Paraphrased.
4   March, vol. 2, no. 9. *Money* (1899).
5   Paraphrased.
6   Pg. 15. *Obama, In His Own Words* (2008), edited by Carl Palmieri.

CHAPTER TWENTY-SIX

Office

John Adams

"My country has contrived for me the most insignificant office that ever the invention of man contrived or his imagination conceived."
—Letter to Mrs. Adams. December 19, 1793.

Thomas Jefferson

"I have no ambition to govern men; it is a painful and thankless office."
—Letter to John Adams. December 28, 1796.

"Whenever a man has cast a longing eye on offices, a rottenness begins in his conduct."
—Letter to Tench Coxe. May 21, 1799.

"The second office in the government is honorable and easy; the first is but a splendid misery."
—Letter to Elbridge Gerry. May 13, 1797.

Andrew Jackson

"The rights of the people have been bartered for promises of office."
—Letter to John Coffee. February 19, 1825.

Martin Van Buren

"As to the presidency, the two happiest days of my life were those of my entrance upon the office and my surrender of it."
—Quoted by Barbara Holland in *Hail to Chiefs* (1990).[1]

James Polk

"The passion for office among members of Congress is very great, if not absolutely disreputable, and greatly embarrasses the operations of the Government. They create offices by their own votes and then seek to fill them themselves."
—Diary. June 22, 1846.

Ulysses Grant

"It was my fortune, or misfortune, to be called to the office of Chief Executive."
—Draft Annual Message to Senate and House of
    Representatives. December 5, 1876.

Rutherford Hayes

"No person connected with me by blood or marriage will be appointed to office."
—Letter to H.S. Noyes. Jul 24, 1878.

"Nothing brings out the lower traits of human nature like office-seeking. Men of good character and impulses are betrayed by it into all sorts of meanness."
—Diary. August 9, 1878.

"I am not liked as a President by the politicians in office. But I am content to abide the judgment the sober second thought of the people."
—Diary. March 1, 1878.

Chester Arthur

"The office of the Vice-President is a greater honor than I ever dreamed of attaining."
—Response to Senator Roscoe Conkling (1880).

Grover Cleveland

"In the scheme of our national government, the presidency is preeminently the people's office."
—In His *Independence of the Executive* (1913).[2]

"Public officers are the servants and agents of the people, to execute the laws which the people have made."
—Letter Accepting the Nomination for Governor of New York. October 7, 1882.

"Officeholders are the agents of the people, not their masters."
—Executive Order. July 14, 1886.

Theodore Roosevelt

"No people are wholly civilized where a distinction is drawn between stealing an office and stealing a purse."
—*The Southwestern Reporter* (1907).[3]

Woodrow Wilson

"When I give a man an office, I watch him carefully to see whether he is swelling or growing."
—Address to the National Press Club. May 15, 1916.

"Every man who takes office in Washington either grows or swells."
　　—Address to the National Press Club. May 15, 1916.

Warren Harding

"I am not fit for this office and should never have been here."
　　—Statement to President of Columbia University, Nicholas
　　　Murray Butler (1923).[4]

Calvin Coolidge

"We need more of the office desk and less of the show window
in politics. Let men in office substitute the midnight oil for the
limelight."
　　—Address at the Home of Augustus Gardner, Hamilton,
　　　Massachusetts. September 1916.

"In the discharge of the duties of this office, there is one rule of
action more important than all others. It consists in never doing
anything that someone else can do for you."
　　—Quoted in *American Magazine* (1929).[5]

Herbert Hoover

"The things I enjoyed most were visits from children. They did
not want public office."
　　—In His Book, *On Growing Up: Letters to American Boys and
　　　Girls* (1962).

"If the law is upheld only by government officials, then all law is
at an end."
　　—State of the Union Address. December 3, 1929.

Franklin Roosevelt

"Let us never forget that government is ourselves and not an
alien power over us. The ultimate rulers of our democracy are

not government officials, but the voters of this country."
—Address at Marietta, Ohio. July 8, 1938.

Harry Truman

"Nixon is one of the few in the history of this country to run for high office talking out of both sides of his mouth at the same time and lying out of both sides."
—*The Bulletin* (1973).[6]

Dwight Eisenhower

"No one should ever sit in this office over 70 years old, and that I know."
—Reported in *Newsweek* (1987).[7]

"The supreme quality for leadership is unquestionably integrity. Without it, no real success is possible in an office."
—Quoted by John Maxwell in *Ultimate Leadership* (2007).[8]

John Kennedy

"When we got into office, the thing that surprised me most was to find that things were just as bad as we'd been saying they were."
—Speech in Washington, D.C. May 27, 1961.

Lyndon Johnson

"There are no favorites in my office. I treat them all with the same general inconsideration."
—*Collier's* (1951).[9]

Bill Clinton

"Poor Darrell Hammond. What's he going to do when I leave office?"
—Address at the Radio and Television Correspondents Association Dinner. April 6, 2000.

Barack Obama

"I found this national debt, doubled, wrapped in a big bow waiting for me as I stepped into the Oval Office."
—Remarks by the President at House Democratic Caucus Issues Conference, Williamsburg, Virginia. February 5, 2009.

1   Pg. 65. *Hail to Chiefs* by Barbara Holland (1990.)
2   Pg. 9. *Independence of the Executive* (1913).
3   Vol. 102. *The Southwestern Reporter* (1907).
4   In Butler's autobiography, *Across the Busy Years* (1932).
5   Vol. 108. *American Magazine* (1929).
6   Vol. 95. part 4. *The Bulletin* (1973).
7   Vol. 18. *Newsweek* (1987).
8   Pg. 286. *Ultimate Leadership* by John Maxwell (2007).
9   Vol. 127, part 1. *Collier's* (1951).

CHAPTER TWENTY-SEVEN

Peace

George Washington

"If we desire to secure peace, it must be known that we are at all times ready for War."
 —Fifth Annual Message. December 3, 1793.

"Observe good faith and justice toward all nations. Cultivate peace and harmony with all."
 —Farewell Address. September 19, 1796.

"To be prepared for war is one of the most effective means of preserving peace."
 —First Annual Message to Congress on the State of the Union. January 8, 1790.

Thomas Jefferson

"Peace and friendship with all mankind is our wisest policy, and I wish we may be permitted to pursue it."
 —Letter to Mr. Dumas. May 6, 1786.

Peace, commerce and honest friendship with all nations; entangling alliances with none.
—First Inaugural Address. March 4, 1801.

Andrew Jackson

"Peace, above all things, is to be desired, but blood must sometimes be spilled to obtain it on equable and lasting terms."
—Quoted in *Edge-Tools of Speech* (1886). [1]

Martin Van Buren

"We remain at peace with all nations."
—First Annual Message. December 5, 1837.

"We decline alliances as adverse to our peace."
—Inaugural Address. March 4, 1837.

James Polk

"May the boldest fear and the wisest tremble when incurring responsibilities on which may depend our country's peace and prosperity, and in some degree the hopes and happiness of the whole human family."
—Inaugural Address. March 4, 1845.

Franklin Pierce

"We have nothing in our history or position to invite aggression; we have everything to beckon us to the cultivation of relations of peace and amity with all nations."
—Inaugural Address. March 4, 1853.

"Cultivate peace and friendship with foreign nations, and demand and exact equal justice from all, but to do wrong to none."
—Second Annual Message. December 4, 1854.

"Never to shrink from war when the rights and the honor of the country call us to arms, but cultivate in preference the arts of peace."
—Second Annual Message. December 4, 1854.

Abraham Lincoln

"Discourage litigation. Persuade your neighbors to compromise whenever you can. As a peacemaker the lawyer has superior opportunity of being a good man."
—Notes for Law Lecture. Circa. July 1, 1850.

"To give victory to the right, not bloody bullets, but peaceful ballots only, are necessary."
—Notes for Speeches. Circa. October 1, 1858.

"Ballots are the rightful and peaceful successors to bullets."
—Special Session Message. July 4, 1861.

Ulysses Grant

"I have never advocated war except as a means of peace."
—Speech in London. June 15, 1877.

"Let us have peace."
—Famous Words during the Civil War, 1861-1865.

James Garfield

"The chief duty of government is to keep the peace and stand out of the sunshine of the people."
—Letter to H. N. Eldridge. December 14, 1869.

Grover Cleveland

"The United States is not a nation to which peace is a necessity."

—Fourth Annual Message (Second Presidential Term).
December 7, 1896.

William McKinley, Jr.

"War should never be entered upon until every agency of peace
has failed."
—Inaugural Address. March 4, 1897.

"Our real eminence rests in the victories of peace, not those of war."
—Address at the Pan-American Exposition, Buffalo, New
York. September 5, 1901.

Theodore Roosevelt

"The things that will destroy America are prosperity-at-any-
price and peace-at-any-price."
—Letter to S. Stanwood Menken. January 10, 1917.

"Wars are, of course, as a rule to be avoided; but they are far bet-
ter than certain kinds of peace."
—Chapter No. 12 in His Book, *Thomas H. Benton*,
Published in 1886.

"If there is not the war, you don't get the great general; if there is
not a great occasion, you don't get a great statesman; if Lincoln
had lived in a time of peace, no one would have known his name."
—Address at the Cambridge Union. May 26, 1910.

"Peace is generally good in itself, but it is never the highest good
unless it comes as the handmaid of righteousness; and it
becomes a very evil thing if it serves merely as a mask for cow-
ardice and sloth, or as an instrument to further the ends of despotism or anarchy."
—Noble Lecture, Oslo, Norway. May 5, 1910.

Calvin Coolidge

"Christmas is not a time nor a season, but a state of mind. To cherish peace and goodwill, to be plenteous in mercy, is to have the real spirit of Christmas."
    —Written Statement from the White House.
      December 25, 1927.

Herbert Hoover

"Peace is not made at the council table or by treaties, but in the hearts of men."
    —Quoted by Alfred Montapert in *Distilled Wisdom* (1964).[2]

Harry Truman

"If you read the history of peace you'll find that there was never a time when there was not extreme danger of war with some foreign power."
    —Letter to Congressman Fallon. November 13, 1951.

"That's all I am trying for: world peace, a lasting peace."
    —Letter to Mr. Littell. Mid-September 1950.

"I would rather have peace in the world than be President."
    —*Life*. Aug 6, 1945.[3]

Dwight Eisenhower

"The people of the world genuinely want peace. Someday the leaders of the world are going to have to give in and give, it to them."
    —Statement to British Prime Minister Harold Macmillan.
      August 31, 1959.[4]

"Though force can protect in emergency, only justice, fairness,

consideration and cooperation can finally lead men to the dawn of eternal peace."
   —*Life*. March 24, 1947.[5]

"Peace and justice are two sides of the same coin."
   —Speech at Columbia University, New York.
      March 23, 1950.

"I like to believe that people in the long run are going to do more to promote peace than our governments."
   —Radio and Television Broadcast With Prime Minister Macmillan in London. August 31, 1959.

"We are going to have peace even if we have to fight for it."
   —*Time*. Jun 25, 1945.

"If men can develop weapons that are so terrifying as to make the thought of global war include almost a sentence for suicide, you would think that man's intelligence and his comprehension would include also his ability to find a peaceful solution."
   —The President's News Conference. November 14, 1956.

"We seek peace, knowing that peace is the climate of freedom."
   —Second Inaugural Address. January 21, 1957.

John Kennedy

"Those who make peaceful revolution impossible will make violent revolution inevitable."
   —Speech on the First Anniversary of the Alliance for Progress. March 13, 1962.

"It is an unfortunate fact that we can secure peace only by preparing for war."
   —Speech Civic Auditorium, Seattle, Washington.
      September 6, 1960.

"Peace is a daily, a weekly, a monthly process, gradually changing opinions, slowly eroding old barriers, quietly building new structures."
—*New World Review* (1963).[6]

Lyndon Johnson

"Peace is a journey of a thousand miles and it must be taken one step at a time."
—Address before the General Assembly of the United Nations. December 17, 1963.

Richard Nixon

"Your steadfastness in supporting our insistence on peace with honor has made peace with honor possible."
—Address to the Nation Announcing Conclusion of an Agreement on Ending the War and Restoring Peace in Vietnam. January 23, 1973.

Jimmy Carter

"War may sometimes be a necessary evil. But no matter how necessary, it is always an evil, never a good. We will not learn how to live together in peace by killing each other's children."
—Nobel Lecture in Oslo, Norway. December 10, 2002.

"We cannot be both the world's leading champion of peace and the world's leading supplier of the weapons of war."
—Statement to Arms Control Association during 1976 Presidential Campaign.

Ronald Reagan

"Peace is not absence of conflict; it is the ability to handle conflict by peaceful means."
—Speech at Eureka College, Illinois. May 9, 1982.

"A people free to choose will always choose peace."
—Address at Moscow State University. May 31, 1988.

George W. Bush

"We know that dictators are quick to choose aggression, while free nations strive to resolve differences in peace."
—Address to the United Nations. September 21, 2004.

"I just want you to know that, when we talk about war, we're really talking about peace."
—Speech at the Department of Housing and Urban Development, Washington, D.C. June 18, 2002.

"We've climbed the mighty mountain. I see the valley below, and it's a valley of peace."
—Presidential Debate in Coral Gables, Florida. September 30, 2004.

"Our aim is a democratic peace—a peace founded upon the dignity and rights of every man and woman."
—Address before a Joint Session of the Congress on the State of the Union. January 20, 2004.

---

1   Ticknor and Co., pg. 361. *Edge-Tools of Speech* (1886).
2   Pg. 271. *Distilled Wisdom* by Alfred Montapert (1964).
3   Pg. 18. *Life*. Aug 6, 1945.
4   An alternate quote of Truman reads, "Indeed, I think that people want peace so much, that one of these days governments had better get out of the way and let them have it."
5   Pg. 89. *Life*. March 24, 1947.
6   Vol. 31. Issue 11. *New World Review* (1963).

CHAPTER TWENTY-EIGHT

Politics

George Washington

"The basis of our political system is the right of the people to make and to alter their constitutions of government."
—Farewell Address. September 19, 1796.

John Adams

"I must not write a word to you about politics, because you are a woman."
—Letter to Abigail Adams. February 13, 1779.

"In politics the middle way is none at all."
—Letter to Horatio Gates. March 23, 1776.

"I must study politics and war that my sons may have liberty to study mathematics and philosophy."
—Letter to Abigail Adams. May 12, 1780.

Thomas Jefferson

"I never considered a difference of opinion in politics as cause for withdrawing from a friend."
　　—Letter to William Hamilton. April 22, 1800.

"Politics is such a torment that I advise everyone I love not to mix with it."
　　—Letter to Martha Jefferson Randolph. February 11, 1800.

James Madison

"There is no maxim which is more liable to be misapplied: the interest of the majority is the political standard of right and wrong."
　　—Letter to Mr. Monroe. October 5, 1786.

Andrew Jackson

"Money is power, and in that government which pays all the public officers of the states will all political power be substantially concentrated."
　　—Veto Message. December 4, 1833.

Andrew Johnson

"We have no angels in the shape of men, as yet, who are willing to take charge of our political affairs."
　　—First Inaugural Address. October 17, 1853.

Rutherford Hayes

"I am not liked as a President by the politicians."
　　—Diary. March 1, 1878.

"The independence of all political and other bothers is happiness."
　　—Diary. March 28, 1875.

Chester Arthur

"What a pleasant lot of fellows they are. What a pity they have so little sense about politics."
  —Statement After a Session With a Number of Democratic Congressmen. Quoted by Thomas Reeves in *Gentleman Boss: The Life of Chester Alan Arthur* (1975).[1]

Grover Cleveland

"Political duty and selfish interests lead in the same direction."
  —Speech at Evacuation Day Celebration, New York. November 26, 1883.

Theodore Roosevelt

"A typical vice of American politics is the avoidance of saying anything real on real issues."
  —*The Outlook*. July 27, 1912.

"The most practical kind of politics is the politics of decency."
  —Statement at Sagamore Hill, Oyster Bay, Long Island. June 1901.

"The most successful politician is he who says what the people are thinking most often in the loudest voice."
  —*Forbes* (1990).[2]

William Taft

"Politics makes me sick."
  —Collection of Private Letters to his Wife.

"I do not know much about politics, but I'm trying the best I can."
  —Quoted by Henry Pringle in *The Life and Times of William Howard Taft* (1939).[3]

"We live in a stage of politics, where legislators seem to regard the passage of laws as much more important than the results of their enforcement."
　　—In His Book, *Our Chief Magistrate and His Powers* (1916).[4]

Woodrow Wilson

"Politics I conceive to be nothing more than the science of the ordered progress of society along the lines of greatest usefulness and convenience to itself."
　　—Address to the Pan-American Scientific Congress.
　　　January 6, 1916.

"My dream of politics all my life has been that it is the common business, that it is something we owe to each other to understand and discuss with absolute frankness."
　　—Campaign Speech of 1912.

Calvin Coolidge

"We need more of the Office Desk and less of the Show Window in politics."
　　—Address at the Home of Augustus Gardner, Hamilton,
　　　Massachusetts. September 1916.

Herbert Hoover

"When we are sick, we want an uncommon doctor; when we have a construction job to do, we want an uncommon engineer, and when we are at war, we want an uncommon general. It is only when we get into politics that we are satisfied with the common man."
　　—Statement as recorded by the U.S. Department of the
　　　Interior.[5]

"Honor is not the exclusive property of any political party."
　　—*Frontier* (1951).[6]

Franklin Roosevelt

"I am neither bitter nor cynical but I do wish there was less immaturity in political thinking."
—Letter to Frank Knox. December 29, 1939.

"In politics, nothing happens by accident. If it happens, you can bet it was planned that way."[7]

Harry Truman

"A President needs political understanding to run the government, but he may be elected without it."
—In His *Memoirs* (1956).[8]

"It's plain hokum. If you can't convince 'em, confuse 'em. It's an old political trick."
—Address at Dexter, Iowa, on the Occasion of the National Plowing Match. September 18, 1948.

"A politician is a man who understands government. A statesman is a politician who's been dead for 15 years."
—Remark at the Reciprocity Club, Washington, D.C. April 11, 1958.

"My choice early in life was either to be a piano-player in a whorehouse or a politician. And to tell the truth, there's hardly any difference."
—*Esquire* (1971).

Dwight Eisenhower

"In most communities it is illegal to cry "fire" in a crowded assembly. Should it not be considered serious international misconduct to manufacture a general war scare in an effort to achieve local political aims?"
—Speech to the Third Special Emergency Session of the General Assembly of the United Nations. August 13, 1958.

"Politics ought to be the part-time profession of every citizen."
—Address Recorded for the Republican Lincoln Day
　　Dinners. January 28, 1954.

"This is battle, this is politics, this is anything."
—The President's News Conference. September 27, 1956

"Politics is a profession; a serious, complicated and, in its true sense, a noble one."
—Letter to Leonard Finder. January 22, 1948.

John Kennedy

"Politics is like football; if you see daylight, go through the hole."
—*New York Herald Tribune*. April 3, 1968.

"I'm always rather nervous about how you talk about women who are active in politics."
—Remarks to a Delegation of Women Assigned to
　　Missions of the United Nations. December 11, 1961.

"Mothers all want their sons to grow up to be president, but they don't want them to become politicians in the process."
—In His Book, *The Strategy for Peace* (1961).[9]

Lyndon Johnson

"I seldom think of politics more than eighteen hours a day."
—Quoted by Kathleen Krull in *Lives of the Presidents* (1998).[10]

"There is ample room for the rich fertility of American political invention."
—Message to Congress. January 12, 1966.

Richard Nixon

"I played by the rules of politics as I found them. Not taking a higher road than my predecessors and adversaries was my central mistake."
—In His Memoir, *In the Arena* (1990).[11]

"I reject the cynical view that politics is a dirty business."
—Address to the Nation about the Watergate Investigations. August 15, 1973.

"Politics would be a helluva good business if it weren't for the goddamned people."
—Private Comment to his Aid. Quoted by Dan Schiller in *Theorizing Communication* (1996).[12]

"The mark of a true politician is that he is never at a loss for words because he is always half-expecting to be asked to make a speech."
—In His Book, *Six Crises* (1962).[13]

Gerald Ford

"I have had a lot of adversaries in my political life, but no enemies that I can remember."
—Statement at the Dedication of the Anderson Independent and Anderson Daily Mail Building in Anderson, South Carolina. October 19, 1974.

Jimmy Carter

"I've never detected any conflict between God's will and my political duty. If you violate one, you violate the other."
—Quoted by Philip Jenkins in *Decade of Nightmares: The End of the Sixties and the Making of Eighties America* (2006).[14]

Ronald Reagan

"It has been said that politics is the second oldest profession. I have learned that it bears a striking resemblance to the first."
—Quoted by Douglas Simpson in *Looking for America* (2006).[15]

"Politics is just like show business. You have a hell of an opening, coast for a while, and then have a hell of a close."
—Comment to Stuart Spencer in 1966.

"Politics is not a bad profession. If you succeed there are many rewards, if you disgrace yourself you can always write a book."
—Quoted by Bob Dole in *Great Presidential Wit* (2001).[16]

George W. Bush

"If you're sick and tired of the politics of cynicism and polls and principles, come and join this campaign."
—Statement at Hilton Head, S.C. February 16, 2000.

Bill Clinton

"One lesson you better learn if you want to be in politics is that you never go out on a golf course and beat the President."
—Remarks during the 2000 President's Cup in Lake Manassas, Virginia. October 18, 2000.

Barack Obama

"In the end, that's what this election is about. Do we participate in a politics of cynicism or a politics of hope?"
—Address at the Democratic National Convention. July 27, 2004.

"That is the true genius of America, a faith in the simple dreams of its people, the insistence on small miracles. That we can say what we think; write what we think, without hearing a sudden knock on the door. That we can have an idea and start our own business without paying a bribe or hearing a sudden knock on the door."

—Speech at the Democratic National Convention. July 27, 2004.

1   Ch. 18. *Gentleman Boss: The Life of Chester Alan Arthur* (1975).
2   Vol. 145. *Forbes* (1990).
3   Vol. 1. *The Life and Times of William Howard Taft* (1939).
4   Pg. 12. *Our Chief Magistrate and His Powers* (1916).
5   www.nps.gov/shen/forteachers/journal-entry-b.htm.
6   Vol. 3. *Frontier* (1951).
7   Scholars debate whether this quote verbatim was uttered by Roosevelt; some say it was actually a misquotation from an address he gave at the Citadel, Charleston, South Carolina on October 23, 1935.
8   Vol. 2. pg. 198. *Memoirs* (1956).
9   Pg. 229. *The Strategy for Peace* (1961).
10 Pg. 72. *Lives of the Presidents* by Kathleen Krull (1998).
11 Pg. 41. *In the Arena* (1990).
12 Pg. 169. by Dan Schiller in *Theorizing Communication* (1996).
13 Pg. 400. *Six Crises* (1962).
14 Pg. 175. *Decade of Nightmares: The End of the Sixties and the Making of Eighties America* by Philip Jenkins (2006).
15 Pg. 55. *Great Presidential Wit* (2001).

CHAPTER TWENTY-NINE

Power

George Washington

"If it was in my power, I would take no advantage of you."
—Letter to Jacob Valentine. November 3, 1797.

"The constitution vests the power of declaring war in Congress."
—Letter to William Moultrie. August 28, 1793.

John Adams

"Because power corrupts, society's demands for moral authority and character increase as the importance of the position increases."
—Quoted by Anthony Hartle in *Moral Issues in Military Decision Making* (1990).

"Power always thinks it has a great soul and vast views beyond the comprehension of the weak."
—Letter to Thomas Jefferson. February 2, 1816.

"Power always thinks that it is doing God's service when it is violating all his laws."
— Letter to Thomas Jefferson. February 2, 1816.

Thomas Jefferson

"I know of no safe depository of the ultimate powers of the society but the people themselves."
— Letter to Mr. Jarvis. September 28, 1820.

"Power is not alluring to pure minds."
— Letter to Mr. Melish. January 13, 1813.

"Power first, and then corruption, it's necessary consequence."
— Letter to Nathaniel Macon. October 20, 1821.

"Even under the best forms of government those entrusted with power have, in time, and by slow operations, perverted it into tyranny."
— In His *Diffusion of Knowledge Bill* (1779).

"I hope our wisdom will grow with our power, and teach us, that the less we use our power the greater it will be."
— Letter to Thomas Leiper. June 12, 1815.

"The constitutions of most of our States assert that all power is inherent in the people."
— Letter to John Cartwright. 1824.

James Madison

"Wherever there is interest and power to do wrong, wrong will generally be done."
— Letter to Thomas Jefferson. October 17, 1788.

"There are more instances of the abridgement of freedom of the people by gradual and silent encroachments by those in power than by violent and sudden usurpations."
—Speech at the Virginia Convention to ratify the Federal Constitution. June 6, 1788.

"The people are the only legitimate fountain of power, and it is from them that the constitutional charter is derived."
—*The Federalist*. February 2, 1788.[1]

"Liberty may be endangered by the abuse of liberty, but also by the abuse of power."
—*The Federalist*, March 1, 1788.

"The essence of Government is power."
—Speech at the Virginia Constitutional Convention. December 2, 1829.

"Power will ever be liable to abuse."
—Speech at the Virginia Constitutional Convention. December 2, 1829.

"All men having power ought to be distrusted to a certain degree."
—Debate. July 11, 1787.

"Where an excess of power prevails, no man is safe."
—Paper on "Property" March. 29, 1792.

John Q. Adams

"Nip the shoots of arbitrary power in the bud, is the only maxim which can ever preserve the liberties of any people."
—*Novanglus Essay*. Published in 1775.[2]

POWER * * * 211

Andrew Jackson

"It is to be regretted that the rich and powerful too often bend the acts of government to their own selfish purposes."
    —Message to Congress. July 10, 1832.

"The people are the government, administering it by their agents; they are the government, the sovereign power."
    —Proclamation 43. December 10, 1832.

"Money is power."
    —Veto Message. December 4, 1833.

Martin Van Buren

"There is a power in public opinion in this country—and I thank God for it: for it is the most honest and best of all powers."
    —Speech at the U.S. Senate. December 5, 1837.

William Harrison

"The only legitimate right to govern is an express grant of power from the governed."
    —Inaugural Address. March 4, 1841.

"There is nothing more corrupting, nothing more destructive of the noblest and finest feelings of our nature, than the exercise of unlimited power."
    —Letter to Bolivar. September 27, 1829.

Zachary Taylor

"The power given by the Constitution to the Executive to interpose his veto should never be exercised except in cases of clear violation of the Constitution."
    —Letter to Capt. J. S. Allison. April 22nd, 1848.

Franklin Pierce

"The dangers of a concentration of all power in the general government of a confederacy so vast as ours are too obvious to be disregarded."
    —Inaugural Address. March 4, 1853.

Abraham Lincoln

"Any people anywhere, being inclined and having the power, have the right to rise up, and shake off the existing government, and form a new one that suits them better. This is a most valuable—a most sacred right—a right, which we hope and believe, is to liberate the world."
    —Speech to House of Representatives. January 12, 1848.

"Nearly all men can stand adversity, but if you want to test a man's character, give him power."
    —Quoted in *The Controller* (1956).[3]

Rutherford Hayes

"The party out of power gains by all partisan conduct of those in power."
    —Diary. March 12, 1878.

James Garfield

"If the power to do hard work is not a skill, it's the best possible substitute for it."
    —*Every Other Sunday* (1900).[4]

Grover Cleveland

"I know He will not turn from us now if we humbly and reverently seek [God's] powerful aid."
    —Inaugural Address, Second Presidential Term. March 4, 1893.

Woodrow Wilson

"The history of liberty is a history of limitations of governmental power, not the increase of it."
  —Speech at New York Press Club. September 9, 1912.

"I have come slowly into possession of such powers as I have."
  —*Papers of Woodrow Wilson* (1888).[5]

Calvin Coolidge

"We do not need more intellectual power, we need more spiritual power."
  —Statement at Wheaton College. Norton, Massachusetts.
    June 19, 1923.

Herbert Hoover

"It is a paradox that every dictator has climbed to power on the ladder of free speech."
  —Quoted by Joslyn Pine in *Wit and Wisdom of the
    American Presidents: A Book of Quotations* (2000).[6]

Franklin Roosevelt

"The ambition of the individual to obtain for him a proper security is an ambition to be preferred to the appetite for great wealth and great power."
  —Message to Congress. January 4, 1935.

Dwight Eisenhower

"The potential for the disastrous rise of misplaced power exists and will persist."
  —Farewell Radio and Television Address to the American
    People. January 17, 1961.

John Kennedy

"I look forward to a great future for America—a future in which our country will match its military strength with our moral restraint, its wealth with our wisdom, its power with our purpose."
  —Remarks at Amherst College upon Receiving an
      Honorary Degree. October 26, 1963.

"We have the power to make this the best generation of mankind in the history of the world—or to make it the last."
  —Address before the 18th General Assembly of the United
      Nations. September 20, 1963.

"Now we have a problem in making our power credible."
  —Statement to Columnist James Reston. March 1961.

"Man holds in his mortal hands the power to abolish all forms of human poverty, as well as all forms of human life."
  —Inaugural Address. January 20, 1961.

"When power leads man toward arrogance, poetry reminds him of his limitations. When power narrows the area of man's concern, poetry reminds him of the richness and diversity of existence. When power corrupts, poetry cleanses."
  —Statement at Amherst College upon Receiving an
      Honorary Degree. October 26, 1963.

"Do not pray for tasks equal to your powers. Pray for powers equal to your tasks."
  —Remarks at the 11th Annual Presidential Prayer
      Breakfast. February 7, 1963.

Ronald Reagan

"Concentrated power has always been the enemy of liberty."
  —Radio Address in 1978.[7]

Bill Clinton

"You are the most powerful cultural force in the world."
　—Remarks with Entertainment and Media Executives on
　　American Ingenuity. February 29, 1996.

George W. Bush

"Use power to help people. For we are given power not to advance our own purposes, nor to make a great show in the world, nor a name."
　—Inaugural Address. January 20, 1989.

"There is but one just use of power and it is to serve people."
　—Inaugural Address. January 20, 1989.

Barack Obama

"What I worry about would be that you essentially have two chambers, the House and the Senate, but you have simply, majoritarian, absolute power on either side. And that's just not what the founders intended."
　—Statement on April 25, 2005.

1　No. 63.
2　No. 3.
3　Vol. 24. *The Controller* (1956).
4　Vol. 16, pg. 40. *Every Other Sunday* (1900).
5　Vol. 6. *Papers of Woodrow Wilson* (1888).
6　Pg. 50. *Wit and Wisdom of the American Presidents: A Book of Quotations* (2000).
7　*Policy Review* (1982). Heritage Foundation, Washington, D.C.

CHAPTER THIRTY

Presidency

Thomas Jefferson

"No man will ever carry out of the Presidency the reputation which carried him into it."
—Letter to Edward Rutledge. December 27, 1796.

Andrew Jackson

"It was settled by the Constitution, the laws, and the whole practice of the government that the entire executive power is vested in the President of the United States."
—Message to the United States Senate. April 15, 1834.

Martin Van Buren

"As to the presidency, the two happiest days of my life were those of my entrance upon the office and my surrender of it."
—Quoted by Barbara Holland in *Hail to Chiefs* (1990).[1]

John Tyler

"If the tide of defamation and abuse shall turn, and my administration comes to be praised, future Vice-Presidents who may succeed to the Presidency may feel some slight encouragement to pursue an independent course."
—Letter to Son, Robert Tyler. March 12, 1848.

James Polk

"No president who performs his duties faithfully and conscientiously can have any leisure."
—Diary. December 29, 1848.

"He should not be the President of a party only, but of the whole people of the United States."
—Inaugural Address. March 4, 1845.

"With me it is exceptionally true that the Presidency is no bed of roses."
—Diary. September 4, 1847.

Zachary Taylor

"The idea that I should become President seems to me too visionary to require a serious answer. It has never entered my head, nor is it likely to enter the head of any other person."
—Letter to Thurlow Weed Shortly after Campaign in Matamoras, Mexico, on April 24, 1847.

Millard Fillmore

"It is a national disgrace that our Presidents, after having occupied the highest position in the country, should be cast adrift, and, perhaps, be compelled to keep a corner grocery for subsistence."
—*New York Herald*. September 16, 1873.

James Buchanan

"Sir, if you are as happy entering the presidency as I am in leaving it, then you are truly a happy man."
    —Statement to Abraham Lincoln on his Presidential Inauguration. March 4, 1861.

"I shall not again be a candidate for the Presidency, for I shall be 65 on the 23rd April next!"
    —During 1856 Presidential Campaigns.

"I am the last President of the United States!"
    —Statement After the Secession of South Carolina on December 20, 1860.

Abraham Lincoln

"Allow the president to invade a neighboring nation, whenever he shall deem it necessary to repel an invasion, and you allow him to do so whenever he may choose to say he deems it necessary for such a purpose—and you allow him to make war at pleasure."
    —Letter to William Herndon. February 15, 1848.

"I shall someday be President of the United States."
    —Statement. Circa. 1830.[2]

Rutherford Hayes

"I am not liked as a President by the politicians in office, in the press, or in Congress."
    —Diary. March 1, 1878.

"The President of the United States should strive to be always mindful of the fact that he serves his party best who serves his country best."
    —Inaugural Address. March 5, 1877.

James Garfield

"The President is the last person in the world to know what the people really want and think."
—As quoted in the *Congressional Quarterly* (1989).

"Few men in our history have ever obtained the Presidency by planning to obtain it."
—Diary. February 4, 1879.

Chester Arthur

"I may be President of the United States, but my private life is nobody's damned business."
—Response to a Temperance Reformer who Asked if He Drank.[3]

"The office of the Vice-President is a greater honor than I ever dreamed of attaining."
—Response to Senator Roscoe Conkling (1880).

"Since I came here I have learned that Chester A. Arthur is one man and the President of the United States is another."
—Statement to Fellow Politicians. Circa. 1882.

Grover Cleveland

"In the scheme of our national government, the presidency is preeminently the people's office."
—In His *Independence of the Executive* (1913).[4]

William McKinley, Jr.

"I have never been in doubt since I was old enough to think intelligently that I would someday be made president."
—Quoted by William Spielman in *William McKinley: A Biographical Study* (1954).

Theodore Roosevelt

"To announce that there must be no criticism of the president is morally treasonable to the American public."
    —*Kansas City Star*. May 7, 1918.

William Taft

"Presidents come and go, but the Supreme Court goes on forever."
    —In *The Yale Law Journal* (1916).[5]

"I am President now, and tired of being kicked around."
    —Statement a Day After His Inauguration. March 5, 1909.

"I have come to the conclusion that the major part of the work of a President is to increase the gate receipts of expositions and fairs and bring tourists to town."
    —Statement Recorded by Archibald Butt in a Letter to Clara
        F. Butt. June 1, 1909.

"I'll be damned if I am not getting tired of this. It seems to be the profession of a President simply to hear other people talk."
    —Quoted by Archibald Butt in *Taft and Roosevelt* (1930).

"The longer I am president the less of a party man I seem to become."
    —Quoted by Archibald Butt in *Taft and Roosevelt* (1930).

Woodrow Wilson

"There are blessed intervals when I forget by one means or another that I am President of the United States."
    —Address to the National Press Club. March 20, 1914.

Calvin Coolidge

"We draw our Presidents from the people. It is a wholesome

thing for them to return to the people. I came from them. I wish to be one of them again."
—In His *The Autobiography Of Calvin Coolidge* (1929).

Herbert Hoover

"The president differs from other men in that he has a more extensive wardrobe."
—*New York Times*. October 17, 1964.

"There are only two occasions when Americans respect privacy, especially in Presidents. Those are prayer and fishing."
—*Let's Go Fishin'*. April 22, 1943.

Franklin Roosevelt

"The ultimate rulers of our democracy are not a President and senators and congressmen and government officials, but the voters of this country."
—Address at Marietta, Ohio. July 8, 1938.

"It is the duty of the President to propose and it is the privilege of the Congress to dispose."
—Press Conference. July 23, 1937.

Harry Truman

"In my opinion eight years as president is enough and sometimes too much for any man to serve in that capacity."
—Diary. April 16, 1950.

"Most of the problems a President has to face have their roots in the past."
—*Life*. January 23, 1956.[6]

"A President needs political understanding to run the govern-

ment, but he may be elected without it."
—In His *Memoirs* (1956).[7]

"All the President is, is a glorified public relations man who spends his time flattering, kissing, and kicking people to get them to do what they are supposed to do anyway."
—Letter to Mary Truman. November 14, 1947.

"If I hadn't been President of the United States, I probably would have ended up a piano player in a bawdy house."
—Statement to Reporters. In Autobiography. 1966.[8]

"It sure is hell to be President."
—Letter to Bess Truman. August 10, 1946.

"I would rather have peace in the world than be President."
—*Life*. Aug 6, 1945.[9]

"A President cannot always be popular."
—In His *Memoirs* (1955).[10]

"If a president isn't in an occasional fight with the Congress or the courts, he's not doing a good job."
—Quoted by Ralph Keyes in *Wit and Wisdom of Harry Truman* (1995).[11]

"A president either is constantly on top of events or, if he hesitates, events will soon be on top of him."
—*Life*. January 23, 1956.

Dwight Eisenhower

"Any man who wants to be president is either an egomaniac or crazy."
—Statement to Executive Director of *New York Herald Tribune*, Bill Robinson. Circa. 1953.

"Unlike presidential administrations, problems rarely have terminal dates."
> —Annual Message to the Congress on the State of the Union. January 12, 1961.

"Well, when you come down to it, I don't see that a reporter could do much to a president, do you?"
> —President's News Conference. January 18, 1961.

John Kennedy

"Mothers all want their sons to grow up to be president, but they don't want them to become politicians in the process."
> —In His book, *The Strategy for Peace* (1961).[12]

"If anyone is crazy enough to want to kill a President of the United States, he can do it."
> —Statement to Pierre Salinger. In Salinger's Biography of the President, *P. S.: A Memoir* (2001).[13]

Lyndon Johnson

"Every President wants to do right."
> —Quoted by Biographer George Christian in *The President Steps Down* (1970).[14]

"Being President is like being a jackass in a hailstorm. There's nothing to do but to stand there and take it."
> —*The Atlantic Monthly* (1973).[15]

"When the burdens of the presidency seem unusually heavy, I always remind myself it could be worse. I could be a mayor."
> —Statement before the National Legislative Conference of the National League of Cities. March 31, 1966.

"The presidency has made every man who occupied it, no matter how small, bigger than he was; and no matter how big, not big enough for its demands."
   —In *United States Code, Congressional, and Administrative News* (1964).[16]

"Whoever won't fight when the President calls him, deserves to be kicked back in his hole and kept there."
   —First Congressional Campaign. March 23, 1937.

"I'm the only President you've got."
   —To Press Corps. Christmas 1964.

"A President's hardest task is not to do what is right, but to know what is right."
   —Annual Message to the Congress on the State of the Union. January 4, 1965.

Richard Nixon

"The presidency has many problems, but boredom is the least of them."
   —Remark. January 1973.

"People have got to know whether or not their president is a crook. Well, I'm not a crook."
   —Q-and-A Session at the Annual Convention of the Associated Press Managing Editors Association, Orlando, Florida. November 17, 1973.

"The American people are entitled to see the president and to hear his views directly, and not to see him only through the press."
   —The President's News Conference. December 10, 1970.

"Unless a president can protect the privacy of the advice he gets, he cannot get the advice he needs."
    —Address to the Nation Announcing Answer to the House Judiciary Committee Subpoena for Additional Presidential Tape Recordings. April 29, 1974.

Gerald Ford

"I am acutely aware that you have not elected me as your President by your ballots, so I ask you to confirm me with your prayers."
    —Address on Taking the Oath of Office. August 9, 1974.

Jimmy Carter

"People make a big fuss over you when you're President. But I'm very serious about doing everything I can to make sure that it doesn't go to my head."
    —*Time* (1977).[17]

Ronald Reagan

"The thought of being President frightens me and I do not think I want the job."
    —In his Biography, *The Reagan Wit* (1993).[18]

"But there are advantages to being elected President. The day after I was elected, I had my high school grades classified Top Secret."
    —Statement. June 19, 1986.

"Thomas Jefferson once said, 'We should never judge a president by his age, only by his works.' And ever since he told me that, I stopped worrying."
    —Address at the Annual Salute to Congress Dinner. February 4, 1981.

"How can a president not be an actor?"
—Quoted by Kenneth Wheeler in *Effective Communication: A Local Government Guide* (1994).

George H. W. Bush

"For seven and a half years I've worked alongside President Reagan. We've had triumphs. Made some mistakes. We've had some sex...uh...setbacks."
—Address at the College of Southern Idaho. May 6, 1988.

"You cannot be President of the United States if you don't have faith. Remember Lincoln, going to his knees in times of trial in the Civil War and all that stuff."
—*Newsweek* (1992).[19]

"I'm going to be so much better a president for having been at the CIA that you're not going to believe it."
—*New York Magazine*. January 21, 1980.[20]

"I'm President of the United States and I'm not going to eat any more broccoli."
—The President's News Conference. March 22, 1990.

Bill Clinton

"You know, everybody makes mistakes when they are President."
—*Newsweek* (2003).[21]

"I haven't eaten at a McDonald's since I became President."
—Interview with Tim Russert. November 9, 1997.

"One lesson you better learn if you want to be in politics is that you never go out on a golf course and beat the President."
—Remarks during the 2000 President's Cup in Lake Manassas, Virginia. October 18, 2000.

"A lot of presidential memoirs, they say, are dull and self-serving. I hope mine is interesting and self-serving."
—*U.S. News & World Report* (2004).[22]

"Being President is like running a cemetery: you've got a lot of people under you and nobody's listening."
—Speech in Galesburg, Illinois. January 30, 1995.

George W. Bush

"I believe the most solemn duty of the American president is to protect the American people."
—Remarks Accepting the Presidential Nomination at the Republican National Convention in New York City. September 2, 2004.

"Do I think faith will be an important part of being a good president? Yes, I do."
—Quoted by US History Site (2006).[23]

Barack Obama

"I don't take a dime of their [lobbyist] money, and when I am president, they won't find a job in my White House."
—Campaign Speech in Spartanburg, South Carolina. November 3, 2007.

1 Pg. 65. ~~Hail to Chiefs~~ (1990).
2 See Arnold, Isaac, *The Life of Abraham Lincoln* (1885).
3 Reeves, Thomas. *Gentleman Boss: The Life of Chester Alan Arthur* (1975), ch. 8.
4 Pg. 9. *Independence of the Executive* (1913).
5 Vol. 25.pg. 616. *The Yale Law Journal* (1916).
6 Pg. 77. *Life*. January 23, 1956.
7 Vol. 2. pg. 198. *Memoirs* (1956).
8 *Good Old Harry: The Wit and Wisdom of Harry S. Truman*. Compiled by George S. Caldwell.
9 Pg. 18. *Life*. Aug 6, 1945.
10 Vol. 2. *Memoirs* (1955).
11 Alternate version: "The President is always abused. If he isn't, he isn't doing anything."

12　Pg. 229. *The Strategy for Peace* (1961).

13　Pg. 155. *P. S.: A Memoir.* By Pierre Salinger (2001).

14　Pg. 41. *The President Steps Down* by George Christian (1970).

15　Vol. 232. *The Atlantic Monthly* (1973).

16　Vol. 2. *United States Code, Congressional, and Administrative News* (1964).

17　Vol. 109. *Time* (1977).

18　Compiled by Bill Adler. *The Reagan Wit* (1993).

19　Vol. 119. *Newsweek* (1992).

20　Pg. 43. *New York Magazine.* January 21, 1980.

21　Vol. 142. *Newsweek* (2003).

22　Vol. 136. *U.S. News & World Report* (2004).

23　See www.ushistorysite.com/index.php.

CHAPTER THIRTY-ONE

Religion

George Washington

"Reason and experience both forbid us to expect that national morality can prevail in exclusion of religious principle."
    —Farewell Address. September 19, 1796.

"Let us with caution indulge the supposition that morality can be maintained without religion."
    —Farewell Address. September 19, 1796.

John Adams

"Our Constitution was made only for a moral and religious people. It is wholly inadequate to the government of any other."
    —Letter to the Officers of the First Brigade of the Third Division of the Militia of Massachusetts. October 11, 1798.

Thomas Jefferson

"I never will, by any word or act, bow to the shrine of intoler-

ance or admit a right of inquiry into the religious opinions of others."
—Letter to Edward Dowse. April 19, 1803.

"I never considered a difference of opinion in religion as cause for withdrawing from a friend."
—Letter to William Hamilton. April 22, 1800.

"The way to silence religious disputes is to take no notice of them."
—*Notes on Virginia* (1782).

"Difference of opinion is advantageous in religion. The several sects perform the office of a Censor—over each other."
—*Notes on the State of Virginia* (1784).[1]

"It is in our lives and not our words that our religion must be read."
—Letter to Mrs. M. Harrison Smith. August 6, 1816.

James Madison

"Religion flourishes in greater purity, without than with the aid of Government."
—Letter to Edward Livingston. July 10, 1822.

"Union of religious sentiments begets a surprising confidence."
—Letter to William Bradford. January 24, 1774.

"Religious bondage shackles and debilitates the mind and unfits it for every noble enterprise, every expanded prospect."
—Letter to Mr. William Bradford, Jr. April 1, 1774.

"Religion and Government will both exist in greater purity, the less they are mixed together."
—Letter to Edward Livingston. July 10, 1822.

John Tyler

"Let it be henceforth proclaimed to the world that man's conscience was created free; that he is no longer accountable to his fellow man for his religious opinions, being responsible therefore only to his God."
—Funeral Oration on the Death of Thomas Jefferson. July 11, 1826.

James Polk

"It becomes us in humility to make our devout acknowledgments to the Supreme Ruler of the Universe for the inestimable civil and religious blessings with which we are favored."
—First Annual Message. December 2, 1845.

Abraham Lincoln

"I care not much for a man's religion whose dog and cat are not the better for it." [2]

"When I do good, I feel good. When I do bad, I feel bad. That's my religion."
—Recalling a Statement by an Attendee at Church in Indiana. Circa. 1810.

Ulysses Grant

"Leave the matter of religion to the family altar, the church, and the private school, supported entirely by private contributions. Keep the church and state forever separate."
—Address to the Army. September 29, 1877.

Woodrow Wilson

"There is no higher religion than human service. To work for the common good is the greatest creed." [3]

"Never at any time teach your child religion dogmatically."[4]
—Address at the Young Men's Christian Association's
Celebration, Pittsburgh, Pennsylvania. October 24, 1914.

Franklin Roosevelt

"Whoever seeks to set one religion against another seeks to destroy all religion."
—Campaign Address at Brooklyn, New York.
November 1, 1940.

John Kennedy

"My religious affiliation is not relevant."
—*Time* (1960).[5]

Richard Nixon

"In the long term we can hope that religion will change the nature of man and reduce conflict. But history is not encouraging in this respect. The bloodiest wars in history have been religious wars."
—In *Real Peace: No more Vietnams* (1990).

Jimmy Carter

"You cannot divorce religious belief and public service."
—Statement to Members of the Southern Baptist Brotherhoo
Commission in Atlanta, Georgia. June 16, 1978.

Ronald Reagan

"Freedom prospers when religion is vibrant and the rule of law under God is acknowledged."
—Statement at the Annual Convention of the National
Association of Evangelicals in Orlando, Florida.
March 8, 1983.

Bill Clinton

"America does not need a religious war. It needs reaffirmation of the values that for most of us are rooted in our religious faith."
  —Speech at University of Notre Dame, South Bend, Indiana. September 11, 1992.

George W. Bush

"There's a certain patience, a certain discipline, I think, that religion helps you achieve."
  —Quoted by Vincent Bzdek in *Woman of the House: The Rise of Nancy Pelosi* (2009).[6]

---

1   Query 17. *Notes on the State of Virginia* (1784).
2   While many sources link this saying to Abraham Lincoln, the quote is also attributed to Rowland Hills.
3   This quote appears to be attributed to several notable historical figures, including Albert Schweitzer and Albert Einstein, in addition to President Wilson. Nevertheless, this quote does justly represent his views, as seen in his Proclamation 1370, delivered on May 18, 1917.
4   Paraphrased.
5   Vol. 76. *Time* (1960).
6   Pg. 55. *Woman of the House: The Rise of Nancy Pelosi* (2009).

CHAPTER THIRTY-TWO

Rights

George Washington

"The basis of our political system is the right of the people to make and to alter their constitutions of government."
—Farewell Address. September 19, 1796.

John Adams

"The right of a nation to kill a tyrant in case of necessity can no more be doubted than to hang a robber, or kill a flea."
—In His *Defense of the Constitutions of Government* (1787).

Thomas Jefferson

"A Bill of Rights is what the people are entitled to against every government, and what no just government should refuse, or rest on inference."
—Letter to James Madison. December 20, 1787.

"Nothing is unchangeable but the inherent and unalienable rights of man."
—Remark to John Cartwright. June 5, 1824.

"All, too, will bear in mind this sacred principle, that though the will of the majority is in all cases to prevail, the minority possess their equal rights, which equal law must protect, and to violate this would be oppression."
—Inaugural Address. March 4, 1801.

"We hold these truths to be self-evident: that all men are created equal; that they are endowed by their Creator with certain unalienable rights; that among these are life, liberty, and the pursuit of happiness."
—Declaration of Independence. July 4, 1776.

James Madison

"The rights of persons, and the rights of property, are the objects, for the protection of which Government was instituted."
—Speech at the Virginia Constitutional Convention.
    December 2, 1829.

"As a man is said to have a right to his property, he may be equally said to have a property in his rights."
—Article on "Property" from His Treatise, *Papers*.
    March 29, 1792.[1]

"In Republics, the great danger is, that the majority may not sufficiently respect the rights of the minority."
—Address at the Virginia Constitutional Convention.
    December 2, 1829.

James Monroe

"The right of self-defense never ceases. It is among the most sacred."
—Second Annual Message. November 17, 1818.

"It is only when our rights are invaded or seriously menaced that we resent injuries or make preparation for our defense."
—Seventh Annual Message. December 2, 1823.

Andrew Jackson

"I weep for the liberty of my country when I see that corruption has been imputed to many members of the House of Representatives, and the rights of the people have been bartered for promises of office."
　　—Letter to John Coffee. February 19, 1825.

"All the rights secured to the citizens under the Constitution are worth nothing, except guaranteed to them by an independent and virtuous Judiciary."
　　—Statement Shortly after Leaving Post of Florida's Military Governorship (1822).[2]

William Harrison

"The only legitimate right to govern is an express grant of power from the governed."
　　—Inaugural Address. March 4, 1841.

James Polk

"One great object of the Constitution was to restrain majorities from oppressing minorities or encroaching upon their just rights."
　　—Inaugural Address. March 4, 1845.

"Minorities have a right to appeal to the Constitution as a shield against oppression."
　　—Inaugural Address. March 4, 1845.

Abraham Lincoln

"Any people anywhere, being inclined and having the power, have the right to rise up, and shake off the existing government, and form a new one that suits them better. This is a most valu-

able—a most sacred right—a right, which we hope and believe, is to liberate the world."
> —Speech to House of Representatives. January 12, 1848.

"He has a right to criticize, who has a heart to help."
> —Quoted in *Forbes* (1960).[3]

"Ballots are the rightful and peaceful successors to bullets."
> —Special Session Message. July 4, 1861.

Calvin Coolidge

"The government of the United States is a device for maintaining in perpetuity the rights of the people, with the ultimate extinction of all privileged classes."
> —Speech on the Anniversary of the First Continental Congress, Philadelphia. September 25, 1924.

"Ultimately property rights and personal rights are the same thing."
> —Address upon Being Elected as President of the Massachusetts Senate. January 7, 1914.

Franklin Roosevelt

"Nobody will ever deprive the American people of the right to vote except the American people themselves."
> —Radio Address from the White House. October 5, 1944.

Lyndon Johnson

"Every man has a right to a Saturday night bath."
> —Quoted by Alice Fleming in *The Senator from Maine* (1976).

"We have talked long enough in this country about equal rights. It is time now to write it in the books of law."
> —Address before a Joint Session of the Congress. November 27, 1963.

"We still have the right to think and speak how we feel."
—Address to the Congressional District. September 15, 1939.

Jimmy Carter

"America did not invent human rights. In a very real sense human rights invented America."
—Farewell Address to the Nation. January 14, 1981.

"Government is a contrivance of human wisdom to provide for human wants. People have the right to expect that these wants will be provided for by this wisdom."
—In His *A Government as Good as Its People* (1996).[4]

"Our commitment to human rights must be absolute, our laws fair; the powerful must not persecute the weak, and human dignity must be enhanced."
—Inaugural Address. January 20, 1977.

"I am not here as a public official, but as a citizen of a troubled world who finds hope in a growing consensus that the generally accepted goals of society are peace, freedom, and human rights."
—Nobel Peace Prize Address. December 10, 2002.

"Human rights is the soul of our foreign policy, because human rights is the very soul of our sense of nationhood."
—Inaugural Address. January 20, 1977.

"Liberty is human rights."
—Farewell Address to the Nation. January 14, 1981.

Ronald Reagan

"Protecting the rights of even the least individual among us is basically the only excuse the government has for even existing."
—Speech during His Governorship of California.
    February 10, 1969.

George W. Bush

"Our aim is a democratic peace—a peace founded upon the dignity and rights of every man and woman."
—Address before a Joint Session of the Congress on the State of the Union. January 20, 2004.

1   14:266-68. *Papers*. March 29, 1792.
2   See: *Journal and Proceedings of the North Carolina State Bar Annual Meeting* (1938), North Carolina State Bar.
3   Vol. 86. *Forbes* (1960).
4   Pg. 5 *A Government as Good as Its People* (1996).

CHAPTER THIRTY-THREE

Success

George Washington

"I attribute all my success in life to the moral, intellectual and physical education I received from my mother."
    —Cited by George W. Bush in his *Proclamation 7674*.
    May 7, 2003.

"Discipline is the soul of an army. It makes small numbers formidable; procures success to the weak, and esteem to all."
    —Letter to the Captains of the Virginia Regiments.
    July 29, 1759.

Abraham Lincoln

"That some achieve great success, is proof to all that others can achieve it as well."
    —Quoted by Steven Stein in *The EQ Edge* (2011).[1]

Grover Cleveland

"A government for the people must depend for its success on the

intelligence, the morality, the justice, and the interest of the people themselves."
—*The Christian Register*. June 23, 1898.

Theodore Roosevelt

"The most important single ingredient in the formula of success is knowing how to get along with people."
—Reported in *Power* (1954).[2]

"Old age is like everything else. To make a success of it, you've got to start young."
—*American Opinion* (1963).[3]

Woodrow Wilson

"Absolute identity with one's cause is the first and great condition of successful leadership."
—*The Virginia Spectator* (1879).[4]

Warren Harding
"The success of our popular government rests wholly upon the correct interpretation of the deliberate, intelligent, dependable popular will of America."
—Inaugural Address. March 4, 1921.

Calvin Coolidge

"If I had permitted my failures, or what seemed to me at the time a lack of success, to discourage me I cannot see any way in which I would ever have made progress."
—Autobiography. 1929.[5]

"Nothing in this world can take the place of persistence. Talent will not; nothing is more common than unsuccessful people with talent. Genius will not; unrewarded genius is almost a proverb."
—*In Locomotive Engineers Journal* (1910).[6]

Dwight Eisenhower

"The supreme quality for leadership is unquestionably integrity. Without it, no real success is possible."
—Quoted by John Maxwell in *Ultimate Leadership* (2007).[7]

Lyndon Johnson

"I don't believe I'll ever get credit for anything I do in foreign affairs no matter how successful it is, because I didn't go to Harvard."
—Quoted by Biographer James Chace in *Acheson: The Secretary of State who Created the American World* (1998).

Bill Clinton

"When I think about the world I would like to leave to my daughter and the grandchildren I hope to have, it is a world that moves away from unequal, unstable, unsustainable interdependence to integrated communities—locally, nationally and globally—that share the characteristics of all successful communities."
—Speech on Rebuilding Rwanda. April 4, 2007.

George W. Bush

"I hope the ambitious realize that they are more likely to succeed with success as opposed to failure."
—Interview with Associated Press. January 18, 2001.

Barack Obama

"In a tolerant America your name is no barrier to success."
—Speech at the Democratic National Convention. July 27, 2004.

---

1   Pg. 233. *The EQ Edge* (2011) by Steven Stein.
2   Vol. 98. *Power* (1954).
3   Vol. 6. *American Opinion* (1963).

4   Pg. 366. *The Virginia Spectator* (1879).
5   *The Autobiography of Calvin Coolidge*, pg. 60.
6   Vol. 44, pg. 1030. *Locomotive Engineers Journal* (1910). Note: Whereas the con-
     tributor in the magazine is shown as "Anonymous," several historians maintain
     that President Coolidge is the source.
7   Pg. 286. by John Maxwell in *Ultimate Leadership* (2007).

CHAPTER THIRTY-FOUR

CHAPTER THIRTY-FOUR

Time

George Washington

"The time is near at hand which must determine whether Americans are to be free men or slaves."
> —Address to Continental Army before Battle of Long
>   Island. August 27, 1776.

Thomas Jefferson

"It takes time to persuade men to do even what is for their own good."
> —Statement to Charles Clay. January 27, 1790.

"Determine never to be idle. No person will have occasion to complain of the want of time who never loses any. It is wonderful how much may be done if we are always doing."
> —Letter to Martha Jefferson. May 5, 1787.

Andrew Jackson

"Take time to deliberate; but when the time for action arrives, stop thinking and go in."
> —*Supplement to the Courant* (1855).[1]

Franklin Pierce

"Remember that time is money."
   —One of the Morals of Chapter Six in His Book, *The Tariff and the Trusts* (1909).

James Buchanan

"Time is a great corrective."
   —Inaugural Address. March 4, 1857.

Abraham Lincoln

"You can fool all the people some of the time, and some of the people all the time, but you cannot fool all the people all the time."
   —Speech in Clinton, Illinois. September 2, 1858.

Theodore Roosevelt

"The only time you really live fully is from thirty to sixty. The young are slaves to dreams; the old servants of regrets. Only the middle-aged have all their five senses in the keeping of their wits."
   —Speech Delivered in Lincoln, Nebraska. June 14, 1917.

"Nine-tenths of wisdom is being wise in time."
   —Speech Delivered in Lincoln, Nebraska. June 14, 1917.

Calvin Coolidge

"They proclaim it can't be done. I deem that the very best time to make the effort."
   —Quoted by President Ronald Reagan in an Address to the National Legislative Conference of the Independent Insurance Agents of America. March 27, 1984.

Herbert Hoover

"About the time we can make the ends meet, somebody moves the ends."
  —Quoted by Ray Baber in *Marriage and the Family* (1953).

Franklin Roosevelt

"It takes a long time to bring the past up to the present."
  —Remarks Pointed toward Ellison Smith during the 1938 Senate Elections.

John Kennedy

"The time to repair the roof is when the sun is shining."
  —State of the Union Address. January 11, 1962.

"We must use time as a tool, not as a couch."
  —Quoted in *Observer*. December 10, 1961.

"Time and the world do not stand still."
  —Speech in the Assembly Hall at Paulskirche in Frankfurt, Germany. June 25, 1963.

Jimmy Carter

"We must adjust to changing times and still hold to unchanging principles."
  —Inaugural Address. January 20, 1977.

Ronald Reagan

"Let us be sure that those who come after will say of us in our time, that in our time we did everything that could be done."
  —Address before a Joint Session of the Congress on the State of the Union. January 25, 1984.

George H. W. Bush

"Because you're burning up time, the meter is running through the sand on you, and I am now filibustering."
—Statement on April 20, 1989.

George W. Bush

"You can fool some of the people all the time, and those are the ones you want to concentrate on."
—Remark in Washington, DC. March 31, 2001.

Barack Obama

"Change will not come if we wait for some other person or some other time."
—Super Tuesday Primaries Speech in Chicago, Illinois. February 5, 2008.

"This is our moment. This is our time."
—Election Victory Speech in Grant Park, Chicago, Illinois. November 4, 2008.

"It's time to fundamentally change the way that we do business in Washington."
—The President's Weekly Address. April 25, 2009.

---

1   Vol. 20-23, pg. 200. *Supplement to the Courant* (1855).

CHAPTER THIRTY-FIVE

Trust

George Washington

"Trust is keeping the enlightened confidence of the people, and by teaching the people themselves to know and to value their own rights." [1]
— First Annual Message to Congress on the State of the Union. January 8, 1790.

John Adams

"Trust no man living with power to endanger the public liberty."
— From His *Notes for an Oration at Braintree*. Spring 1772.

Thomas Jefferson

"Men may be trusted to govern themselves without a master."
— Letter to David Hartley. July 2, 1787.

"Whenever the people are well-informed, they can be trusted with their own government."
— Richard Price. January 8, 1789.

"Sometimes it is said that man cannot be trusted with the government of himself. Can he, then, be trusted with the government of others? Or have we found angels in the form of kings to govern him? Let history answer this question."
—Inaugural Address. March 4, 1801.

"When a man assumes a public trust he should consider himself a public property."
—Conversation with Baron Humboldt in 1807.

"Every government degenerates when trusted to the rulers of the people alone. The people themselves are its only safe depositories."
—In His *Notes on Virginia* (1782).

"Experience hath shown, that even under the best forms of government those entrusted with power have, in time, and by slow operations, perverted it into tyranny."
—In His *Diffusion Of Knowledge Bill* (1779).

James Madison

"All men having power ought to be distrusted to a certain degree."
—Debate. July 11, 1787.

Millard Fillmore

"The man who can look upon a crisis without being willing to offer himself upon the altar of his country is not fit for public trust."
—Speech in Louisville, Kentucky. March 15, 1854.

Ulysses Grant

"I have made it a rule of my life to trust a man long after other people gave him up."
—Remarks in Court Deliberations during the Spring of 1885.

"The friend in my adversity I shall always cherish most. I can better trust those who helped to relieve the gloom of my dark hours than those who are so ready to enjoy with me the sunshine of my prosperity."
    —Quoted in *Forbes* (1960).[2]

Grover Cleveland

"Your every voter exercises a public trust."
    —Inaugural Address. March 4, 1885.

Calvin Coolidge

"Those who trust to chance must abide by the results of chance."
    —In *American Magazine* (1932).[3]

Harry Truman

"The human animal cannot be trusted for anything good except en masse."
    —Memo. May 22, 1945.

Dwight Eisenhower

"This world of ours must avoid becoming a community of dreadful fear and hate, and be, instead, a proud confederation of mutual trust and respect."
    —Farewell Address to the Nation. January 17, 1961.

"History does not long entrust the care of freedom to the weak or the timid."
    —Inaugural Address. January 20, 1953.

John Kennedy

"We are not afraid to entrust the American people."
    —Remarks on the 20th Anniversary of the Voice of America. February 26, 1962.

Lyndon Johnson

"What we won when all of our people united must not be lost in suspicion and distrust."
—Diary Entry. March 31, 1968.

Ronald Reagan

"Trust, but verify."
—Remark at the Signing of the INF Treaty, Washington, D.C. December 8, 1987.

George W. Bush

"Just trust me."
—During a Discussion on the National Economy in Bakersfield, California. March 4, 2004.

Barack Obama

"If the people cannot trust their government to do the job for which it exists—to protect them and to promote their common welfare—all else is lost."
—Speech at the University of Nairobi. August 28, 2006.

1   Paraphrased.
2   Vol. 86. *Forbes* (1960).
3   Vol. 69. *American Magazine* (1932).

CHAPTER THIRTY-SIX

Truth

George Washington

"Actions, not words, are the true criterion."
  —Letter to Major-General Sullivan. December 15, 1779.

"Truth will ultimately prevail where there is pains to bring it to light."
  —Letter to Charles Thruston. August 10, 1794.

Thomas Jefferson

"The advertisement is the most truthful part of a newspaper."
  —Quoted in *Marketing/Communications* (1898).[1]

"I was bold in the pursuit of knowledge, never fearing to follow truth and reason to whatever results they led."
  —Letter to Dr. Thomas Cooper. February 10, 1814.

"Truth is certainly a branch of morality and a very important one to society."
  —Letter to Thomas Law. June 13, 1814.

"Advertisements contain the only truths to be relied on in a newspaper."
 —Letter to Nathaniel Macon. January 12, 1819.

"He who knows nothing is closer to the truth than he whose mind is filled with falsehoods and errors."
 —Letter to John Norvell. June 11, 1807.

"Ignorance is preferable to error, and he is less remote from the truth who believes nothing than he who believes what is wrong."
 —In *Notes on the State of Virginia* (1782).

"There is not a truth existing which I fear or would wish unknown to the whole world."
 —Letter to Henry Lee. May 15, 1826.

"We hold these truths to be self-evident: that all men are created equal; that they are endowed by their Creator with certain unalienable rights; that among these are life, liberty, and the pursuit of happiness."
 —Declaration of Independence. July 4, 1776.

"In truth, politeness is artificial good humor."
 —Letter to his Grandson, Thomas Jefferson Randolph. November 24, 1808.

"Truth can stand by itself."
 —In *Notes on the State of Virginia* (1782).

James Madison

"If we are to take for the criterion of truth the majority of suffrages, they ought to be gotten from those philosophic and patriotic citizens who cultivate their reason."
 —To Dr. Rush. March 7, 1790.

"It is a universal truth that the loss of liberty at home is to be charged to the provisions against danger, real or pretended, from abroad."
   —Letter to Thomas Jefferson. May 13, 1798.

"All men having power ought to be distrusted to a certain degree."
   —Debate. July 11, 1787.

William Harrison

"Sir, I wish to understand the true principles of the Government. I wish them carried out. I ask nothing more."
   —Last Words before His Death. April 4, 1841.[2]

James Polk

"With me it is exceptionally true that the Presidency is no bed of roses."
   —Diary. September 4, 1847.

Abraham Lincoln

"There is nothing true anywhere, The true is nowhere to be seen; If you say you see the true, This seeing is not the true one."
   —Quoted by Thomas Wallin in *Lincoln's Quotes and My Limericks* (2010).[3]

"I am a firm believer in the people. If given the truth, they can be depended upon to meet any national crisis."
   —Speech to House of Representatives. January 12, 1848.[4]

"I am not bound to win, but I am bound to be true."
   —Quoted by Horace Platt in *John Marshall and Other Addresses* (1908).[5]

"Truth is the daughter of Time."
  —Statement. Circa. 1850.[6]

Rutherford Hayes

"The truth is, this being errand boy to one hundred and fifty thousand people tires me so by night I am ready for bed instead of soirees."
  —Diary. January 10, 1866.

James Garfield

"The truth will set you free, but first it will make you miserable."
  —Quoted by Henry Ivey in *Two Sides of the River: A Time to Choose* (2011).[7]

Grover Cleveland

"I would rather the man who presents something for my consideration subject me to a zephyr of truth and a gentle breeze of responsibility rather than blow me down with a curtain of hot wind."
  —As Quoted by the Grover Cleveland Library (2006).[8]

"A truly American sentiment recognizes the dignity of labor and the fact that honor lies in honest toil."
  —Letter Accepting Nomination of the U.S. Presidency. August, 18, 1884.

Benjamin Harrison

"The bud of victory is always in the truth."
  —Speech in Indianapolis, Indiana. September 18, 1888.

William Taft

"Don't worry over what the newspapers say. I don't. Why should anyone else? I told the truth to the newspaper correspondents—

but when you tell the truth to them they are at sea."
   —Remark to a Reporter in 1909. [9]

Woodrow Wilson

"He is not a true man of the world who knows only the present fashions of it."
   —Address at the Princeton Sesqui-Centennial Celebration.
      October 21, 1896.

Franklin Roosevelt

"The truth is found when men are free to pursue it."
   —Upon receiving an Honorary Degree from Temple
      University, Philadelphia. February 22, 1936.

Harry Truman

"I never did give anybody hell, I just told the truth."
   —Statement to Edward R. Murrow in 1958.

"Intense feeling too often obscures the truth."
   —Address at Raleigh, North Carolina. October 19, 1948.

"My choice early in life was either to be a piano-player in a whorehouse or a politician. And to tell the truth, there's hardly any difference."
   —*Esquire* (1971).

John Kennedy

"For a nation that is afraid to let its people judge the truth and falsehood in an open market is a nation that is afraid of its people."
   —Remarks on the 20th Anniversary of the Voice of
      America. February 26, 1962.

"The great enemy of the truth is very often not the lie, but the myth."
— Commencement Address at Yale University. June 11, 1962.

"The goal of education is the advancement of knowledge and the dissemination of truth."
— Speech at Harvard University. June 14, 1956.

Richard Nixon

"People react to fear, not love; they don't teach that in Sunday School, but it's true."
— Quoted by William Safire in *Before the Fall* (1977).[10]

Gerald Ford

"Tell the truth, work hard, and come to dinner on time."
— From His Memoir, *A Time to Heal* (1979).

"Truth is the glue that holds government together."
— Statement on Taking the Oath of Office. August 9, 1974.

Ronald Reagan

"It's true hard work never killed anybody, but I figure, why take the chance?"
— Statement at the Gridiron Dinner, March 28, 1987.

Barack Obama

"That is the true genius of America, a faith in the simple dreams of its people, the insistence on small miracles. That we can say what we think, write what we think, without hearing a sudden knock on the door. That we can have an idea and start our own business without paying a bribe or hearing a sudden knock on the door."
— Speech at the Democratic National Convention.
    July 27, 2004.

"It's only when you hitch your wagon to something larger than yourself that you realize your true potential."
  —Commencement Address at Knox College, Galesburg, Illinois. June 4, 2005.

1   Vol. 22, pg. 18. *Marketing/Communications* (1898).
2   Quoted by Jebediah Whitman in *A Memorial to Our Dear Departed President* (1841).
3   Pg. 114. *Lincoln's Quotes and My Limericks* (2010).
4   Although this particular quote is also said to be attributed to Douglas MacArthur, the quote matches the sentiment of Lincoln's speech.
5   Pg. 208. by Horace Platt in *John Marshall and Other Addresses* (1908).
6   This particular quote has been uttered by several personalities throughout history, including Sir Francis Bacon and Aulus Gellius.
7   Pg. 210. by Henry Ivey in *Two Sides of the River: A Time to Choose* (2011).
8   See http://groverclevelandlibrary.org/Intro.html.
9   See Henry Pringle, *The Life and Times of William Howard Taft* (1939).
10 Pg. 8. *Before the Fall* (1977) by William Safire.

CHAPTER THIRTY-SEVEN

War

George Washington

"My first wish is to see this plague of mankind, war, banished from the earth."
 —Letter to David Humphreys. July 25, 1785.

"If we desire to avoid insult, we must be able to repel it; if we desire to secure peace, one of the most powerful instruments of our rising prosperity, it must be known, that we are at all times ready for War."
 —Fifth Annual Message. December 3, 1793.

"To be prepared for war is one of the most effective means of preserving peace."
 —First Annual Message to Congress on the State of the Union. January 8, 1790.

"War—An act of violence whose object is to constrain the enemy, to accomplish our will."
 —Collection of Letters to Tobias Lear and Others. Dated 1790-1799.[1]

John Adams

"Great is the guilt of an unnecessary war."
— Letter to Abigail Adams. May 19, 1794.

"I must study politics and war that my sons may have liberty to study mathematics and philosophy."
— Letter to Abigail Adams. May 12, 1780.

Thomas Jefferson

"The most successful war seldom pays for its losses."
— Letter to Edmund Randolph. September 20, 1785.

"I abhor war and view it as the greatest scourge of mankind."
— Letter to Elbridge Gerry. May 13, 1797.

"It is our duty still to endeavor to avoid war; but if it shall actually take place, no matter by whom brought on, we must defend ourselves. If our house be on fire, without inquiring whether it was fired from within or without, we must try to extinguish it."
— Letter to James Lewis, Jr. May 9, 1798.

"War is an instrument entirely inefficient toward redressing wrong; and multiplies, instead of indemnifying, losses."
— Letter to John Sinclair. March 23, 1798.

"I have seen enough of one war never to wish to see another."
— Letter to John Adams. April 25, 1794.

James Madison

"Of all the enemies of public liberty, war is perhaps the most to be dreaded, because it comprises and develops the germ of every other."
— *Political Observations*. April 20, 1795.

"No nation could preserve its freedom in the midst of continual warfare."

—*Political Observations*. April 20, 1795.

"Each generation should be made to bear the burden of its own wars, instead of carrying them on, at the expense of other generations."

—*Universal Peace Essay*. January 31, 1792.

"War contains so much folly, as well as wickedness, that much is to be hoped from the progress of reason."

—*Universal Peace Essay*. January 31, 1792.

"War should only be declared by the authority of the people, whose toils and treasures are to support its burdens, instead of the government which is to reap its fruits."

—*Universal Peace Essay*. January 31, 1792.

James Monroe

"Preparation for war is a constant stimulus to suspicion and ill will."

—Letter to Secretary of State, Paris. January 26, 1796.[2]

"It is only when our rights are invaded or seriously menaced that we resent injuries or make preparation for our defense."

—Seventh Annual Message. December 2, 1823.

Franklin Pierce

"Never shrink from war when the rights and the honor of the country call us to arms, but cultivate in preference the arts of peace."

—Second Annual Message. December 4, 1854.

Andrew Jackson

"War is a blessing compared with national degradation."
  —Letter to James Polk. May 2, 1845.

"Gallows ought to be the fate of all such ambitious men who would involve their country in civil wars."
  —Letter to Rev. A. J. Crawford. May 1, 1833.

Abraham Lincoln

"Allow the president to invade a neighboring nation, whenever he shall deem it necessary to repel an invasion, and you allow him to do so whenever he may choose to say he deems it necessary for such a purpose- and you allow him to make war at pleasure."
  —Letter to William Herndon. February 15, 1848.

Ulysses Grant

"I have never advocated war except as a means of peace."
  —Speech in London. June 15, 1877.

"Although a soldier by profession, I have never felt any sort of fondness for war."
  —Speech in London. June 15, 1877.

"If men make war in slavish obedience to rules, they will fail."
  —Conversation with John Russell Young in 1879.

"Wars produce many stories of fiction, some of which are told until they are believed to be true."
  —Personal Memoir. 1885.

"The art of war is simple enough. Find out where your enemy

is. Get at him as soon as you can. Strike him as hard as you can, and keep moving on."
    —Statement to John Brinton at the Start of the Tennessee
        River Campaign. Early 1862.[3]

Rutherford Hayes

"Wars will remain while human nature remains."
    —Diary. August, 11, 1890.

James Garfield

"Ideas are the great warriors of the world, and a war that has no idea behind it, is simply a brutality."
    —Memoirs. 1881.

"The reply to war is not words but swords."
    —Memoirs. 1881.

"Battles are never the end of war."
    —Memoirs. 1881.

William McKinley, Jr.

"Let us ever remember that our interest is in concord, not in conflict; and that our real eminence rests in the victories of peace, not those of war. "
    —Address at the Pan-American Exposition, Buffalo,
        New York. September 5, 1901.

"War should never be entered upon until every agency of peace has failed."
    —Inaugural Address. March 4, 1897.

Theodore Roosevelt

"If there is not the war, you don't get the great general; if there

is not a great occasion, you don't get a great statesman; if Lincoln had lived in a time of peace, no one would have known his name."
   —Address at the Cambridge Union. May 26, 1910.

"Wars are, of course, as a rule to be avoided; but they are far better than certain kinds of peace."
   —Chapter No. 12 in His Book, *Thomas H. Benton*, Published in 1886.

Calvin Coolidge

"No nation ever had an army large enough to guarantee it against attack in time of peace or to insure its victory in time of war."
   —Address before the American Legion Convention at Omaha, Nebraska. October 6, 1925.

Herbert Hoover

"It is youth who must inherit the tribulation, the sorrow and the triumphs that are the aftermath of war."
   —Speech at the 23rd Republican National Convention, Chicago, Illinois. June 27, 1944.

"Older men declare war. But it is the youth that must fight and die."
   —Speech at the 23rd Republican National Convention, Chicago, Illinois. June 27, 1944.

Franklin Roosevelt

"More than an end to war, we want an end to the beginning of all wars—yes, an end to this brutal, inhuman and thoroughly impractical method of settling the differences between governments."
   —Undelivered Address Prepared for Jefferson Day. April 13, 1945.

"Don't forget what I discovered that over ninety percent of all national deficits from 1921 to 1939 were caused by payments for past, present, and future wars."
   —Letter to Adolph Berle, Jr. June 21, 1941.

"War is a contagion."
   —"Quarantine the Aggressors" Address. Chicago, Illinois. October 5, 1937.

Dwight Eisenhower

"I hate war as only a soldier who has lived it can, only as one who has seen its brutality, its futility, its stupidity."
   —Speech in Ottawa, Canada. January, 10 1946.

"When people speak to you about a preventive war, you tell them to go and fight it. After my experience, I have come to hate war."
   —*Quote*. April 4, 1965.

"If men can develop weapons that are so terrifying as to make the thought of global war include almost a sentence for suicide, you would think that man's intelligence and his comprehension would include also his ability to find a peaceful solution.
   —The President's News Conference. November 14, 1956.

"War settles nothing."
   —*Quote*. April 4, 1965.

John Kennedy

"Unconditional war can no longer lead to unconditional victory. It can no longer serve to settle disputes. It can no longer be of concern to great powers alone."
   —Address before the General Assembly of the United Nations, New York City. September 25, 1961.

"War will exist until that distant day when the conscientious objector enjoys the same reputation and prestige that the warrior does today."
—Letter to Navy Friend in 1945.

"It is an unfortunate fact that we can secure peace only by preparing for war."
—Speech Civic Auditorium, Seattle, Washington. September 6, 1960.

"Mankind must put an end to war before war puts an end to mankind."
—Address before the General Assembly of the United Nations, New York City. September 25, 1961.

Lyndon Johnson

"The last thing I wanted to do was to be a wartime President."
—*Readers' Digest*. February 1969.

Jimmy Carter

"We cannot be both the world's leading champion of peace and the world's leading supplier of the weapons of war."
—Statement to Arms Control Association during 1976 Presidential Campaign.

"War may sometimes be a necessary evil. But no matter how necessary, it is always an evil, never a good. We will not learn how to live together in peace by killing each other's children."
—Nobel Lecture in Oslo, Norway. December 10, 2002.

Ronald Reagan

"History teaches that war begins when governments believe the price of aggression is cheap."
—Address from the White House on United States-Soviet Relations. January 16, 1984.

"People do not make wars; governments do."
—Session With Students and Faculty at Moscow State
University. May 31, 1988.

Bill Clinton

"Just as war is freedom's cost, disagreement is freedom's privilege."
—Remark at a Memorial Day Ceremony at the Vietnam
Veterans Memorial. May 31, 1993.

"America does not need a religious war."
—Speech at University of Notre Dame, South Bend,
Indiana. September 11, 1992.

"Democracies don't go to war against each other."
—Speech at Georgetown University, Washington D.C.
December 12, 1991.

"Democracies don't attack each other."
—State of the Union Address. January 25, 1994.

George W. Bush

"I just want you to know that, when we talk about war, we're
really talking about peace."
—Speech at the Department of Housing and Urban
Development, Washington, D.C. June 18, 2002.

Barack Obama

"I don't oppose all wars. What I am opposed to is a dumb war.
What I am opposed to is a rash war."
—Remarks Against Going to War in Iraq. October 2, 2002.

1   This quote, verbatim or in likeness, has been known to be recited by George Washington on numerous occasions. The content in these letters embody this quote's essence.
2   This saying is widely attributed to James Monroe, and embodies the meaning of this particular letter.
3   See: https://www.cia.gov/library/publications/additional-publications/civil-war/p16.htm.

CHAPTER THIRTY-EIGHT

Wisdom

George Washington

"The success of Government depends on wise measures." [1]
— Inaugural Address. April 30, 1789.

"It will be found an unjust and unwise jealousy to deprive a man of his natural liberty upon the supposition he may abuse it." [2]

"Let us raise a standard to which the wise and honest can repair; the rest is in the hands of God."
— Quoted by Gerald Ford during a speech to the Summit Conference on Inflation. September 28, 1974.

Thomas Jefferson

"Beauty is jealous, and ill bears the presence of a rival. But Wisdom I know is social. She seeks her fellows."
— Letter to Abigail Adams. September, 25, 1785.

"Peace and friendship with all mankind is our wisest policy, and I wish we may be permitted to pursue it."
— Letter to Mr. Dumas. May 6, 1786.

"A wise and frugal government, which shall leave men free to regulate their own pursuits of industry and improvement, and shall not take from the mouth of labor the bread it has earned—this is the sum of good government."
—Inaugural Address. March 4, 1801.

"So confident am I in the intentions, as well as wisdom, of the government, that I shall always be satisfied that what is not done, either cannot, or ought not to be done."
—Letter to James Madison. June 21, 1813.

"I hope our wisdom will grow with our power, and teach us, that the less we use our power the greater it will be."
—Letter to Thomas Leiper. June 12, 1815.

"Honesty is the first chapter in the book of wisdom."
—Letter to Nathaniel Macon. January 12, 1819.

James Madison

"Every nation whose affairs betray a want of wisdom and stability may calculate on every loss which can be sustained from the more systematic policy of its wiser neighbors."
—In His *The Federalist*.[3] February 27, 1788.

Andrew Jackson

"The wisdom of man never yet contrived a system of taxation that would operate with perfect equality."
—Proclamation 43, on Nullifying Laws of South Carolina. December 10, 1832.

James Polk

"May the boldest fear and the wisest tremble when incurring

responsibilities on which may depend our country's peace and prosperity."
   —Inaugural Address. March 4, 1845.

James Buchanan

"To avoid entangling alliances has been a maxim of our policy ever since the days of Washington, and its wisdom no one will attempt to dispute."
   —Inaugural Address. March 4, 1857.

Abraham Lincoln

"I do not think much of a man who is not wiser today than he was yesterday."
   —Address at the Republican State Convention in
      Springfield, Illinois. June 16, 1858.

Andrew Johnson

"Legislation can neither be wise nor just which seeks the welfare of a single interest at the expense and to the injury of many and varied interests."
   —Message to the House of Representatives.
      February 22, 1869.

James Garfield

"All free governments are managed by the combined wisdom and folly of the people."
   —Letter to B. A. Hinsdale. April 21, 1880.

Theodore Roosevelt

"Nine-tenths of wisdom is being wise in time."
   —Speech Delivered in Lincoln, Nebraska. June 14, 1917.

Calvin Coolidge

"Knowledge comes, but wisdom lingers."
—Speech before the Graduating Class, U.S. Naval
Academy, Annapolis, Maryland, June 3, 1925.

Herbert Hoover

"Wisdom consists not so much in knowing what to do in the ultimate as knowing what to do next."
—In *Forbes* (1923).

Dwight Eisenhower

"Neither a wise man nor a brave man lies down on the tracks of history to wait for the train of the future to run over him."
—*Time*. October 6, 1952.

"The older I get the more wisdom I find in the ancient rule of taking first things first. A process which often reduces the most complex human problem to a manageable proportion."
—*Saturday Review* (1966).[4]

John Kennedy

"I look forward to a great future for America—a future in which our country will match its military strength with our moral restraint, its wealth with our wisdom, its power with our purpose."
—Remarks at Amherst College Upon Receiving an
Honorary Degree. October 26, 1963.

Jimmy Carter

"Government is a contrivance of human wisdom to provide for human wants. People have the right to expect that these wants will be provided for by this wisdom."
—In His *A Government as Good as Its People* (1996).[5]

Bill Clinton

"Strength and wisdom are not opposing values."
—Address to Democratic National Convention.
July 27, 2004.

Barack Obama

"We need earmark reform, and when I'm President, I will go line by line to make sure that we are not spending money unwisely."
—Presidential Debate at the University of Mississippi.
September 26, 2008.

---

1   Paraphrased.
2   Although commonly attributed to Washington (as in Glen Beck's *Seven Wonders That Will Change Your Life*, 2011) this quote was actually written by Oliver Cromwell in a letter to the governor of Edinburgh Castle on September 12, 1650. That being said, this quote does embody Washington's disposition to liberty being the birthright for every individual.
3   No. 62. *The Federalist*. February 27, 1788.
4   Vol. 49. *Saturday Review*. 1966. Also see *Debates of the Senate: Official Report* (2003).
5   Pg. 5. *A Government as Good as Its People* (1996).

CHAPTER THIRTY-NINE

Wish

George Washington

"My first wish is to see this plague of mankind, war, banished from the earth."
—Letter to David Humphreys. July 25, 1785.

"Lenience will operate with greater force, in some instances than rigor. It is therefore my wish to have all of my conduct distinguished by it."
—Quoted in *Maxims of Washington*[1] (1894).[2]

"I can only say that there is not a man living who wishes more sincerely than I do to see a plan adopted for the abolition of slavery."
—Letter to Robert Morris. April 12, 1786.

John Adams

"Facts are stubborn things; and whatever may be our wishes, they cannot alter the state of facts and evidence."
—Statement during the Boston Massacre Trials.
December 4, 1770.

Thomas Jefferson

"The spirit of resistance to government is so valuable on certain occasions that I wish it to be always kept alive."
　　—Letter to Abigail Adams. February 22, 1787.

"Peace and friendship with all mankind is our wisest policy, and I wish we may be permitted to pursue it."
　　—Letter to Mr. Dumas. May 6, 1786.

"An enemy generally says and believes what he wishes."
　　—Letter to Mr. Dumas. March 29, 1788.

"There is not a truth existing which I fear or would wish unknown to the whole world."
　　—Letter to Henry Lee. May 15, 1826.

"I have seen enough of one war never to wish to see another."
　　—Letter to John Adams. April 25, 1794.

Andrew Jackson

"I am a Senator against my wishes and feelings, which I regret more than any other of my life."
　　—In a Collection of Letters Dating to April 30, 1814.

"You must pay the price if you wish to secure the blessing."
　　—Farewell Address. March 4, 1837.

William Harrison

"Sir, I wish to understand the true principles of the Government. I wish them carried out. I ask nothing more."
　　—Last Words before His Death. April 4, 1841.[3]

Abraham Lincoln

"The way for a young man to rise is to improve himself in every way he can, never suspecting that anybody wishes to hinder him."
—Letter to William Herndon. July 10, 1848.

Theodore Roosevelt

"I wish to preach, not the doctrine of ignoble ease, but the doctrine of the strenuous life."
—Speech before the Hamilton Club, Chicago, Illinois. April 10, 1899.

Woodrow Wilson

"America lives in the heart of every man everywhere who wishes to find a region where he will be free to work out his destiny as he chooses."
—Campaign Speech, Chicago, Illinois. April 6, 1912.

Calvin Coolidge

"We draw our Presidents from the people. It is a wholesome thing for them to return to the people. I came from them. I wish to be one of them again."
—In His *The Autobiography Of Calvin Coolidge* (1929).

"I sometimes wish that people would put a little more emphasis upon the observance of the law than they do upon its enforcement."
—Autobiography. 1924.[4]

Franklin Roosevelt

"I am neither bitter nor cynical but I do wish there was less immaturity in political thinking."
—Letter to Frank Knox, Dec. 29, 1939.

Dwight Eisenhower

"Pull the string, and it will follow wherever you wish. Push it, and it will go nowhere at all."
—Quoted in *The Landman* (1988).[5]

John Kennedy

"Let every nation know, whether it wishes us well or ill, that we shall pay any price, bear any burden, meet any hardship, support any friend, oppose any foe to assure the survival and the success of liberty."
—Inaugural Address. January 20, 1961.

Lyndon Johnson

"This is a moment that I deeply wish my parents could have lived to share. My father would have enjoyed what you have so generously said of me- and my mother would have believed it."
—In His *The Johnson Wit* (1965).[6]

Richard Nixon

"I wish I could give you a lot of advice, but I don't have that experience."
—Letter to Robert Gray. Circa. 1967.

Bill Clinton

"We must do unto all men as you wish to have done to you and reject for others what you would reject for yourself."
—Address at Holy Eucharist Services. January 2, 2000.

George W. Bush

"It's a real treat to be able to walk around the halls of a success-

ful school and, most importantly, be able to look children in the eye and wish them all the best."
— Remarks at Merritt Extended Elementary School.
   January 25, 2001.

Barack Obama

"I wish there was a forum or policy that can bring back all the jobs we've lost overnight."
— The President's Weekly Address. November 21, 2009.

1   Compiled by D. Appleton and Co.
2   Pg. 335. *Maxims of Washington* (1894).
3   Quoted by Jebediah Whitman in *A Memorial to Our Dear Departed President* (1841).
4   *Calvin Coolidge, His Ideals of Citizenship As Revealed Through his Speeches and Writings* (W. A. Wilde Company), pg. 30.
5   Vol. 33. *The Landman* (1988).
6   Pg. 14. *The Johnson Wit* (1965).

CHAPTER FORTY

World

George Washington

"A slender acquaintance with the world must convince every man that actions, not words, are the true criterion of the attachment of friends."
　　—Letter to Major-General Sullivan. December 15, 1779.

Thomas Jefferson

"I find that he is happiest of whom the world says least, good or bad."
　　—Letter to John Adams. August 27, 1786.

"The good opinion of mankind moves the world."
　　—Letter to Jose Correa da Serra. December 27, 1814.

"There is not a truth existing which I fear or would wish unknown to the whole world."
　　—Letter to Henry Lee. May 15, 1826.

"It is incumbent on every generation to pay its own debts as it goes. A principle which if acted on would save one-half the wars of the world."
　　—Letter to Destutt Tracy. December 26, 1820.

"Whenever you do a thing, act as if all the world were watching."
　　—Quoted by Gary McDowell in *Reason and Republicanism: Thomas Jefferson's Legacy of Liberty* (1997).[1]

James Madison

"The happy Union of these States is a wonder; their Constitution a miracle; their example the hope of Liberty throughout the world."
　　—Letter to Samuel Kercheval. September 7, 1829.

"The world is indebted for all the triumphs which have been gained by reason and humanity over error and oppression."
　　—Report on the Virginia Resolutions at the Session of 1799-1800.

"Let me recommend the best medicine in the world: a long journey, at a mild season, through a pleasant country, in easy stages."
　　—Letter to Horatio Gates. February 23, 1794.

Andrew Jackson

"No one need think that the world can be ruled without blood. The civil sword shall and must be red and bloody."
　　—Statement Made during Tenure as Florida's Military Governor. Circa. 1821.[2]

Martin Van Buren

"Those who have wrought great changes in the world never succeeded by gaining over chiefs; but always by exciting the multitude."
　　—*The New Monthly*. January 1823.[3]

John Tyler

"Let it be henceforth proclaimed to the world that man's conscience was created free."
   —Funeral Oration on the Death of Thomas Jefferson.
      July 11, 1826.

James Polk

"Peace, plenty, and contentment reign throughout our borders, and our beloved country presents a sublime moral spectacle to the world."
   —Fourth Annual Message. December 5, 1848.

"The world has nothing to fear from military ambition in our Government."
   —Inaugural Address. March 4, 1845.

James Buchanan

"Liberty must be allowed to work out its natural results; and these will, ere long, astonish the world."
   —Letter to Mr. Slidell. November 10, 1845.

Abraham Lincoln

"Any people anywhere, being inclined and having the power, have the right to rise up, and shake off the existing government, and form a new one that suits them better. This is a most valuable—a most sacred right—a right, which we hope and believe, is to liberate the world."
   —Speech to House of Representatives. January 12, 1848.

"Common looking people are the best in the world: that is the reason the Lord makes so many of them."
   —Conversation with Secretary John Hay.
      December 23, 1863.

Rutherford Hayes

"The progress of society is mainly the improvement in the condition of the workingmen of the world."
—Diary. February 27, 1890.

James Garfield

"The President is the last person in the world to know what the people really want and think."
—As Quoted in the *Congressional Quarterly* (1989).

"Things don't turn up in this world until somebody turns them up."
—Address to the House of Representatives. June 23, 1874.

"Ideas are the great warriors of the world."
—Memoirs. 1881.

"Ideas are the great warriors of the world."
—Speech to the House of Representatives. August 4, 1876.

Benjamin Harrison

"We Americans have no commission from God to police the world."
—Statement to Congress in 1888.[4]

William Taft

"The world is not going to be saved by legislation."
—In His Book, *Our Chief Magistrate and His Powers* (1916).[5]

Woodrow Wilson

"You are not here merely to make a living. You are here in order to enable the world to live more amply."
—Address at Swarthmore College. October 25, 1913.

"You are here to enrich the world."
— Address at Swarthmore College. October 25, 1913.

"He is not a true man of the world who knows only the present fashions of it."
— Address at the Princeton Sesqui-Centennial Celebration. October 21, 1896.

"I am not sure that it is of the first importance that you should be happy. Many an unhappy man has been of deep service to himself and to the world."
— Address at Princeton University. June 7, 1908.

"America is the only idealistic nation in the world."
— Address at Sioux Falls. September 8, 1919.

"The world must be made safe for democracy."
— Address to Congress for a Declaration of War against Germany. April 2, 1917.

"There is little for the great part of the history of the world except the bitter tears of pity and the hot tears of wrath."
— Speech in Oakland, California. September 18, 1919.

"The world is not looking for servants, there are plenty of these, but for masters, men who form their purposes and then carry them out."
— Collection of Papers Written between 1907 and 1908.[6]

"Nothing in this world can take the place of persistence."
— In *Locomotive Engineers Journal* (1910).[7]

Franklin Roosevelt

"If civilization is to survive, we must cultivate the science of

human relationships—the ability of all peoples, of all kinds, to live together, in the same world at peace."
—Undelivered Jefferson Day Address. April 13, 1945.

"We have always held to the hope, the belief, the conviction that there is a better life, a better world, beyond the horizon."
—Address. Oct. 12, 1940.

"The world will either move forward toward unity and widely shared prosperity- or it will move apart."
—Message to Congress. February 12, 1945.

Harry Truman

"I do not believe there is a problem in this country or the world today which could not be settled if approached through the teaching of the Sermon on the Mount."
—Speech Delivered at the Lighting of the National Community Christmas Tree, Washington, D.C. December 24, 1945.

"The White House is the finest prison in the world."
—Frequently-Made Statement. Alluded to This in His Presidential Notes Dating from 1949.

"There is nothing new in the world except the history you do not know."
—In His *Mr. President* (1952).[8]

"I would rather have peace in the world than be President."
—*Life*. Aug 6, 1945.[9]

Dwight Eisenhower

"The free world must now prove itself worthy of its own past."
—In *What Eisenhower Thinks* (1952).

"This world of ours must avoid becoming a community of dreadful fear and hate, and be, instead, a proud confederation of mutual trust and respect."
—Farewell Address to the Nation. January 17, 1961.

"The people of the world genuinely want peace."
—Statement to British Prime Minister Harold Macmillan. August 31, 1959.[10]

"The world moves, and ideas that were once good are not always good."
—Statement during Press Conference. Washington D.C. August 31, 1955.

"Whatever America hopes to bring to pass in the world must first come to pass in the heart of America."
—Inaugural Address. January 20, 1953.

John Kennedy

"We prefer world law in the age of self-determination to world war in the age of mass extermination."
—Speech before the General Assembly of the United Nations. New York City. September 25, 1961.

"The problems of the world cannot possibly be solved by skeptics or cynics whose horizons are limited by the obvious realities. We need men who can dream of things that never were."
—Speech before the Irish Parliament, Dublin. June 28, 1963.

"In the long history of the world, only a few generations have been granted the role of defending freedom in its hour of maximum danger. I do not shrink from this responsibility—I welcome it."
—Inaugural Address. January 20, 1961.

"We have the power to make this the best generation of mankind in the history of the world-- or to make it the last."
   —Address before the 18th General Assembly of the United Nations. September 20, 1963.

"The world is very different now. For man holds in his mortal hands the power to abolish all forms of human poverty, and all forms of human life."
   —Inaugural Address. January 20, 1961.

"Time and the world do not stand still."
   —Speech in the Assembly Hall at Paulskirche in Frankfurt, Germany. June 25, 1963.

"The basic problems facing the world today are not susceptible to a military solution."
   —Special Message to the Congress on the Defense Budget. March 28, 1961.

"If we cannot now end our differences, at least we can help make the world safe for diversity."
   —Address in Amherst College, Massachusetts. October 26, 1963.

Lyndon Johnson

"I am concerned about the whole man. I am concerned about what the people, using their government as an instrument and a tool, can do toward building the whole man, which will mean a better society and a better world."
   —Statement on Medical Research. April 13, 1963.

"We live in a world that has narrowed into a neighborhood before it has broadened into a brotherhood."
   —Speech at the Lighting of the Nation's Christmas Tree. December 22, 1963.

"If future generations are to remember us more with gratitude than sorrow, we must achieve more than just the miracles of technology. We must also leave them a glimpse of the world as it was created, not just as it looked when we got through with it."
    —Statement at the Signing of a Bill Establishing the Assateague Island Seashore National Park. September 21, 1965.

Jimmy Carter

"We cannot be both the world's leading champion of peace and the world's leading supplier of the weapons of war."
    —Statement to Arms Control Association during 1976 Presidential Campaign.

"Globalization, as defined by rich people like us, is a very nice thing. You are talking about the Internet, you are talking about cell phones, you are talking about computers. This doesn't affect two-thirds of the people of the world."
    —*Congressional Record*. October 6, 2004.

Ronald Reagan

"We must realize that no weapon in the arsenals of the world, is so formidable as the will and moral courage of free men and women."
    —Inaugural Address. January 20, 1981.

"We cannot play innocents abroad in a world that is not innocent."
    —Address before a Joint Session of the Congress on the State of the Union. February 6, 1985.

"They say the world has become too complex for simple answers. They are wrong."
    —Speech on Behalf of Republican Party Nominee Barry Goldwater. October 27, 1964.

George H. W. Bush

"We don't want an America that is closed to the world. What we want is a world that is open to America."
   —Remarks at the Swearing-in Ceremony for Carla A. Hills as United States Trade Representative. February 6, 1989.

"America is never wholly herself unless she is engaged in high moral principle. We as a people have such a purpose today. It is to make kinder the face of the nation and gentler the face of the world."
   —Inaugural Address. January 20, 1989.

Bill Clinton

"You are the most powerful cultural force in the world."
   —Remarks With Entertainment and Media Executives on American Ingenuity. February 29, 1996.

George W. Bush

"If America shows weakness and uncertainty, the world will drift toward tragedy. That will not happen on my watch."
   —Remarks to the Republican Governors Association. February 23, 2004.

"Make sure that the world we leave behind is a better place for all."
   —Address to United States Military Personnel in Baghdad. June 13, 2006.

"We will stand up for our friends in the world."
   —Statement to the American Jewish Committee. May 3, 2001.

"We will build new ships to carry man forward into the universe, to gain a new foothold on the moon and to prepare for new journeys to the worlds beyond our own."
   —Address on a New Vision for Space Exploration. January 14, 2004.

Barack Obama

"Let us resolve that we will not leave our children a world where the oceans rise and famine spreads and terrible storms devastate our lands."
—Speech in Berlin, Germany. July 24, 2008.

"We've made our share of mistakes, and there are times when our actions around the world have not lived up to our best intentions."
—Speech in Berlin, Germany. July 24, 2008.

"We have real enemies in the world, and they must be found."
—Keynote Address at the 2004 Democratic National Convention. Tuesday, July 27, 2004.

"People of the world—this is our moment. This is our time."
—Speech in Berlin, Germany. July 24, 2008.

"Today we begin in earnest the work of making sure that the world we leave our children is just a little bit better than the one we inhabit today."
—From the *Office of the President* (2012).[11]

1   Pg. 284. *Reason and Republicanism: Thomas Jefferson's Legacy of Liberty* (1997).
2   This particular quote was delivered by Martin Luther in his pamphlet, *On Trade and Usury* (1524). Nevertheless, several scholars claim President Jackson, quipped "Old Hickory" and "Sharp Knife" by his contemporaries, quoted Luther in his own words to express his own sentiments, as evidenced by his heavy involvement in expeditions ranging from the American Revolutionary War to the Seminole Wars of the 1800s.
3   Vol. 5, pg. 288. *The New Monthly*. January 1823.
4   Caroline T. Hamsberger, *Treasury of Presidential Quotations* (1964).
5   Pg. 13. *Our Chief Magistrate and His Powers* (1916).
6   *The Papers of Woodrow Wilson* (1974), edited by Arthur S. Link.
7   Vol. 44, pg. 1030. *Locomotive Engineers Journal* (1910). Note: Whereas the contributor in the magazine is shown as "Anonymous," several historians maintain that President Coolidge is the source.
8   Pg. 81. *Mr. President* (1952).

9   Pg. 18. *Life*. Aug 6, 1945.
10 An alternate quote of Truman reads, "Indeed, I think that people want peace so much, that one of these days governments had better get out of the way and let them have it."
11 See Obama-Biden Transition Project: http://change.gov.

ACKNOWLEDGMENTS

Wisdom from the Oval Office is currently the largest collection of presidential quotations available in the literary market. Compiling this work of honor could not be possible without acknowledging the contributions of a few individuals.

First and foremost, I would like to thank my agent, Claire Gerus, for her continuing support, direction, and patience, and her superb skills in representing me and my work. I also would like to express appreciation to the History Publishing Company, who helped transform an abstract idea into the lively, revealing pages that *Wisdom from the Oval Office* encompasses today. Special thanks to president Don Bracken, editor Carolyn Winters, and designer Robert Aulicino.

Last but not least, I would like to sincerely thank my parents, who always urged me to follow my dreams, and my wife, without whom my dreams would only be a fantasy.

INDEX

Adams, John
  on America, 2
  on Constitution, 32-33
  on country, 41
  on democracy, 50
  on education, 63
  on freedom, 72-73
  on friendship, 84
  on God, 95
  on government, 102-103
  on happiness, 122
  on hope, 137
  on law, 142
  on liberty, 154
  on life, 161
  on love, 171
  on mind, 174
  on money, 180
  on office, 185
  on politics, 199
  on power, 208-209
  on religion, 229
  on rights, 234
  on trust, 248
  on war, 260
  on wish, 274
Adams, John Q.
  on America, 3
  on freedom, 74
  on friendship, 86
  on hope, 138
  on leadership, 148
  on liberty, 156
  on power, 210
Arthur, Chester
  on freedom, 76
  on friendship, 88
  on honor, 135

  on life, 164
  on money, 183
  on office, 187
  on politics, 201
  on presidency, 219

Buchanan, James
  on America, 3
  on Constitution, 35
  on country, 44
  on democracy, 51
  on freedom, 75
  on friendship, 87
  on happiness, 124
  on leadership, 148
  on liberty, 157
  on presidency, 218
  on time, 245
  on wisdom, 271
  on world, 281
Bush, George H. W.
  on America, 16
  on Constitution, 38
  on country, 49
  on democracy, 55
  on freedom, 81
  on friendship, 93
  on history, 133
  on honor, 136
  on leadership, 151
  on presidency, 226
  on time, 247
  on world, 288
Bush, George W.
  on America, 16-18
  on belief, 22-23
  on business, 26
  on change, 31

on Constitution, 39
on country, 49
on democracy, 56
on economy, 62
on education, 68
on freedom, 82
on friendship, 93
on God, 100
on government, 120
on history, 133
on hope, 140-141
on law, 147
on leadership, 151
on liberty, 160
on life, 169
on money, 184
on peace, 198
on politics, 206
on power, 215
on presidency, 227
on religion, 233
on rights, 239
on success, 242
on time, 247
on trust, 251
on war, 267
on wish, 277-278
on world, 288

Carter, Jimmy
on America, 14-15
on belief, 22
on change, 30
on Constitution, 37
on democracy, 54
on freedom, 80
on friendship, 92
on God, 99
on government, 117
on happiness, 125
on history, 132
on hope, 140

on leadership, 151
on liberty, 160
on life, 168
on peace, 197
on politics, 205
on presidency, 225
on religion, 232
on rights, 238
on time, 246
on war, 266
on wisdom, 272
on world, 287

Cleveland, Grover
on America, 4
on country, 45-46
on democracy, 52
on friendship, 88-89
on government, 111-112
on honor, 135
on law, 144
on mind, 176-177
on office, 187
on peace, 193-194
on politics, 201
on power, 212
on presidency, 219
on success, 240-241
on trust, 250
on truth, 255

Clinton, Bill
on America, 16
on change, 31
on Constitution, 38-39
on country, 49
on democracy, 55
on economy, 61
on education, 67-68
on freedom, 81
on friendship, 93
on God, 99
on government, 119
on office, 189

on politics, 206
on power, 215
on presidency, 226-227
on religion, 233
on success, 242
on war, 267
on wisdom, 273
on wish, 277
on world, 288
Coolidge, Calvin
on America, 7
on business, 25
on Constitution, 36
on country, 47
on democracy, 53
on economy, 59
on friendship, 90
on government, 114
on honor, 135
on hope, 139
on law, 145-146
on life, 165
on office, 188
on peace, 195
on politics, 202
on power, 213
on presidency, 220-221
on rights, 237
on success, 241
on time, 245
on trust, 250
on war, 264
on wisdom, 272
on wish, 276

Eisenhower, Dwight
on America, 10
on belief, 22
on country, 47-48
on freedom, 78-79
on friendship, 91
on government, 116

on history, 130
on hope, 139
on law, 146
on leadership, 149-150
on liberty, 159
on life, 166
on office, 189
on peace, 195-196
on politics, 203-204
on power, 213
on presidency, 222-223
on success, 242
on trust, 250
on war, 265
on wisdom, 272
on wish, 277
on world, 284-285

Fillmore, Millard
on change, 29
on country, 44
on freedom, 75
on friendship, 87
on God, 97
on government, 109
on honor, 135
on presidency, 217
on trust, 249
Ford, Gerald
on America, 14
on Constitution, 36
on democracy, 54
on friendship, 92
on government, 117
on history, 132
on hope, 140
on law, 147
on love, 172-173
on politics, 205
on presidency, 225
on truth, 257

Garfield, James
  on country, 45
  on education, 65
  on freedom, 76
  on government, 111
  on history, 128
  on law, 144
  on life, 163
  on money, 183
  on peace, 193
  on power, 212
  on presidency, 219
  on truth, 255
  on war, 263
  on wisdom, 271
  on world, 282
Grant, Ulysses
  on error, 70
  on friendship, 88
  on law, 144
  on office, 186
  on peace, 193
  on religion, 231
  on trust, 249-250
  on war, 262-263

Harding, Warren
  on America, 6-7
  on democracy, 53
  on friendship, 90
  on God, 98
  on government, 113-114
  on office, 188
  on success, 241
Harrison, Benjamin
  on America, 4
  on change, 29
  on freedom, 76
  on friendship, 89
  on God, 98
  on government, 112
  on history, 128

  on life, 164
  on truth, 255
  on world, 282
Harrison, William
  on freedom, 75
  on friendship, 86
  on government, 108-109
  on power, 211
  on rights, 236
  on truth, 254
  on wish, 275
Hayes, Rutherford
  on business, 25
  on country, 45
  on education, 64
  on friendship, 88
  on God, 98
  on happiness, 125
  on hope, 138
  on law, 144
  on life, 163
  on office, 186-187
  on politics, 200
  on power, 212
  on presidency, 218
  on truth, 255
  on war, 263
  on world, 282
Hoover, Herbert
  on America, 7-8
  on business, 25
  on change, 29
  on economy, 59
  on error, 70
  on freedom, 77-78
  on friendship, 90
  on government, 114
  on honor, 136
  on hope, 139
  on law, 146
  on money, 183
  on office, 188

on peace, 195
on politics, 202
on power, 213
on presidency, 221
on time, 246
on war, 264
on wisdom, 272

Jackson, Andrew
on America, 3
on belief, 20-21
on business, 24
on Constitution, 34
on country, 43
on democracy, 51
on economy, 58
on error, 70
on freedom, 75
on friendship, 86
on government, 107-108
on honor, 135
on law, 143
on liberty, 157
on life, 162
on love, 171
on money, 181-182
on office, 186
on peace, 192
on politics, 200
on power, 211
on presidency, 216
on rights, 236
on time, 244
on war, 262
on wisdom, 270
on wish, 275
on world, 280
Jefferson, Thomas
on America, 2
on belief, 20
on change, 28
on Constitution, 33

on country, 42
on democracy, 50-51
on education, 63-64
on error, 69-70
on freedom, 73-74
on friendship, 84-85
on God, 95-96
on government, 103-105
on happiness, 122-123
on history, 127
on honor, 134
on hope, 137-138
on law, 142
on liberty, 154-155
on life, 161-162
on mind, 174-175
on money, 180-181
on office, 185
on peace, 191-192
on politics, 200
on power, 209
on presidency, 216
on religion, 229-230
on rights, 234-235
on time, 244
on trust, 248-249
on truth, 252-253
on war, 260
on wisdom, 269-270
on wish, 275
on world, 279-280
Johnson, Andrew
on Constitution, 35
on country, 45
on economy, 58
on friendship, 88
on government, 111
on law, 143-144
on mind, 176
on politics, 200
on wisdom, 271
Johnson, Lyndon

on America, 12-13
on belief, 22
on Constitution, 36
on country, 48
on economy, 61
on education, 67
on error, 71
on freedom, 80
on friendship, 92
on God, 98-99
on government, 116
on happiness, 125
on history, 131
on law, 146
on life, 167-168
on office, 189
on peace, 197
on politics, 204
on presidency, 223-224
on rights, 237-238
on success, 242
on trust, 251
on war, 266
on wish, 277
on world, 286-287

Kennedy, John
on America, 11-12
on business, 26
on change, 30
on country, 48
on democracy, 54
on economy, 60-61
on education, 66-67
on freedom, 79-80
on friendship, 91
on God, 98
on government, 116
on history, 130-131
on hope, 140
on law, 146
on leadership, 150

on liberty, 159
on life, 166-167
on mind, 178
on office, 189
on peace, 196-197
on politics, 204
on power, 214
on presidency, 223
on religion, 232
on time, 246
on trust, 250
on truth, 256-257
on war, 265-266
on wisdom, 272
on wish, 277
on world, 285-286

Lincoln, Abraham
on America, 4
on belief, 21
on Constitution, 35
on country, 45
on democracy, 52
on freedom, 75-76
on friendship, 88
on God, 97
on government, 110-111
on happiness, 124-125
on hope, 138
on law, 143
on liberty, 157
on life, 163
on love, 172
on mind, 175-176
on money, 182-183
on peace, 193
on power, 212
on presidency, 218
on religion, 231
on rights, 236-237
on success, 240
on time, 245

on truth, 254-255
on war, 262
on wisdom, 271
on wish, 276
on world, 281

Madison, James
on America, 3
on Constitution, 33
on country, 42
on democracy, 51
on education, 64
on error, 70
on freedom, 74
on friendship, 85
on government, 105-106
on happiness, 123-124
on history, 127
on hope, 138
on law, 143
on liberty, 155-156
on mind, 175
on money, 181
on politics, 200
on power, 209-210
on religion, 230
on rights, 235
on trust, 249
on truth, 253-254
on war, 260-261
on wisdom, 270
on world, 280
McKinley, William, Jr.
on freedom, 77
on friendship, 89
on history, 128
on hope, 139
on life, 164
on peace, 194
on presidency, 219
on war, 263
Monroe, James

on country, 42
on friendship, 86
on government, 106-107
on happiness, 124
on history, 128
on honor, 134
on liberty, 156
on rights, 235
on war, 261

Nixon, Richard
on America, 13-14
on change, 30
on friendship, 92
on government, 116-117
on history, 131-132
on honor, 136
on leadership, 150-151
on love, 172
on peace, 197
on politics, 205
on presidency, 224-225
on religion, 232
on truth, 257
on wish, 277

Obama, Barack
on America, 18-19
on belief, 23
on business, 27
on change, 31
on Constitution, 39-40
on country, 49
on democracy, 56-57
on economy, 62
on education, 68
on freedom, 82
on friendship, 93-94
on God, 100
on government, 120
on hope, 141
on leadership, 151-152

on liberty, 160
on life, 169-170
on love, 173
on money, 184
on office, 190
on politics, 206-207
on power, 215
on presidency, 227
on success, 242
on time, 247
on trust, 251
on truth, 257-258
on war, 267
on wisdom, 273
on wish, 278
on world, 289

Pierce, Franklin
  on Constitution, 34
  on democracy, 51
  on economy, 58
  on friendship, 87
  on God, 97
  on government, 109-110
  on history, 128
  on money, 182
  on peace, 192-193
  on power, 212
  on time, 245
  on war, 261
Polk, James
  on Constitution, 34
  on country, 43-44
  on God, 96
  on government, 109
  on happiness, 124
  on office, 186
  on peace, 192
  on presidency, 217
  on religion, 231
  on rights, 236
  on truth, 254

on wisdom, 270-271
on world, 281

Reagan, Ronald
  on America, 15
  on business, 26
  on change, 31
  on Constitution, 37
  on country, 48
  on democracy, 54-55
  on economy, 61
  on freedom, 80-81
  on friendship, 92
  on God, 99
  on government, 117-119
  on history, 132
  on hope, 140
  on law, 147
  on liberty, 160
  on life, 168-169
  on love, 173
  on mind, 178
  on money, 184
  on peace, 197-198
  on politics, 206
  on power, 214
  on presidency, 225-226
  on religion, 232
  on rights, 238
  on time, 246
  on trust, 251
  on truth, 257
  on war, 266-267
  on world, 287
Roosevelt, Franklin
  on America, 8-9
  on belief, 21
  on business, 26
  on change, 29
  on Constitution, 36
  on country, 47
  on democracy, 53

on economy, 59-60
on education, 65-66
on freedom, 78
on friendship, 90-91
on government, 115
on happiness, 125
on history, 129
on honor, 136
on hope, 139
on law, 146
on liberty, 159
on life, 165-166
on love, 172
on mind, 177
on office, 188-189
on politics, 203
on power, 213
on presidency, 221
on religion, 232
on rights, 237
on time, 246
on truth, 256
on war, 264-265
on wish, 276
on world, 283-284
Roosevelt, Theodore
on America, 4-5
on belief, 21
on country, 46
on education, 65
on freedom, 77
on friendship, 89
on government, 112
on history, 128-129
on honor, 135
on law, 145
on leadership, 148-149
on liberty, 158
on life, 164-165
on love, 172
on mind, 177
on office, 187

on peace, 194
on politics, 201
on presidency, 220
on success, 241
on time, 245
on war, 263-264
on wisdom, 271
on wish, 276
Taft, William
on America, 5
on country, 46
on friendship, 89
on God, 98
on government, 112
on law, 145
on love, 172
on politics, 201-202
on presidency, 220
on truth, 255-256
on world, 282
Taylor, Zachary
on Constitution, 34
on country, 44
on friendship, 87
on power, 211
on presidency, 217
Truman, Harry
on America, 9
on belief, 21-22
on change, 30
on country, 47
on economy, 60
on education, 66
on freedom, 78
on friendship, 91
on government, 115-116
on history, 129-130
on leadership, 149
on life, 166
on mind, 177-178
on office, 189
on peace, 195

on politics, 203
on presidency, 221-222
on trust, 250
on truth, 256
on world, 284
Tyler, John
on economy, 58
on freedom, 75
on friendship, 87
on God, 96
on government, 109
on presidency, 217
on religion, 231
on world, 281

Van Buren, Martin
on business, 24
on change, 28
on country, 43
on friendship, 86
on God, 96
on government, 108
on happiness, 124
on law, 143
on life, 163
on money, 182
on office, 186
on peace, 192
on power, 211
on presidency, 216
on world, 280

Washington, George
on America, 1
on business, 24
on Constitution, 32
on country, 41
on democracy, 50
on education, 63
on error, 69
on freedom, 72
on friendship, 84

on God, 95
on government, 101-102
on happiness, 122
on history, 127
on honor, 134
on hope, 137
on liberty, 153
on life, 161
on peace, 191
on politics, 199
on power, 208
on religion, 229
on rights, 234
on success, 240
on time, 244
on trust, 248
on truth, 252
on war, 259
on wisdom, 269
on wish, 274
on world, 279
Wilson, Woodrow
on America, 5-6
on business, 25
on change, 29
on country, 46-47
on democracy, 52
on education, 65
on freedom, 77
on friendship, 89
on God, 98
on government, 113
on happiness, 125
on history, 129
on hope, 139
on law, 145
on leadership, 149
on liberty, 158
on life, 165
on love, 172
on office, 187-188
on politics, 202

on power, 213
on presidency, 220
on religion, 231-232
on success, 241
on truth, 256
on wish, 276
on world, 282-283